TOUGH TALK 2

We dedicate this book to our wives –
Denise, Carol and Lynda

TOUGH TALK 2

with Millie Murray

Authentic

This edition published 2008 by Authentic Media
Reprinted 2012, 2017 by Authentic Media Limited
PO Box 6326, Bletchley, Milton Keynes MK1 9GG
www.authenticmedia.co.uk

British Library Cataloguing in Publication Data
A catalogue record for this book is available from the British Library

ISBN 978-1-86024-700-2

Some of the names in these stories have been changed to protect
people involved

Cover Design by David Lund
Printed and bound in Great Britain by CPI Group (UK) Ltd, Croydon, CR0 4YY

Contents

Contents

Foreword

It is now more than a decade since Tough Talk was formed and the three founder members of the team started to share the dramatic stories of their journeys to faith in Jesus Christ. In 2000, these three men published their stories in the book *Tough Talk*. This book has been very popular and has been read by thousands of people and reprinted several times.

However, over the years the membership of the team has changed – new men have joined who also have powerful stories to tell. Therefore, this book has been produced to present the stories of three of the newer members of the current team.

As Chairman of the Trustees and the team's administrator, I have had the privilege of knowing these men since they joined the team and have heard their stories and observed their lives. These three genuine stories from three genuine men are very different but have a common theme. Each life has been dramatically changed from one that was spiralling out of control because of a number of factors including drugs, alcohol, selfishness, greed and violence, to a life that has peace, hope, purpose and direction.

The message behind these stories is that anyone, irrespective of their background and past mistakes, can have a totally new start in their life.

I unreservedly recommend it.

Professor Michael Steward, Chairman of Trustees

Introduction

'. . . You've heard what these guys have said, how Jesus has dramatically changed their lives.'

The auditorium was packed with at least a hundred people who had come to listen to the men of Tough Talk tell the story of their changed lives. The summer evening was sweltering. I felt overwhelmed with the heat, and the deep emotions that the guys had once again stirred within me, as I heard the miracle of God working through their lives. They had just finished giving their stories and lifting the heavy weights and now I stood in front of them on the platform addressing the people who had come to hear them.

'Maybe you think that the guys' stories are good, but it's got nothing to do with you? The Bible tells us that everyone has made mistakes. Nobody's perfect, and you may think that because you haven't murdered anyone or done something "really bad", you're OK. Well, Jesus Himself said that anyone who calls his brother a "fool" will incur the wrath of God and, without repentance and acceptance of Christ, is in danger of the fire of hell.

'The good news is that no matter what you've done, Jesus will never condemn you. Rather, Jesus says, "Whoever comes to me, I will never turn away." That

means you – ' I pointed to a man in the crowd. Then I
jabbed my finger at different people who were in the
congregation, 'you, you and you . . . And me. We can all
receive God's love and mercy and have our sins completely done away with. All this is what God offers and
has been freely given to us because of what Christ suffered on the cross, for you and me.

'You've heard these guys' tremendous accounts of
how Jesus has changed their lives . . . ' I took a deep
breath and turned to face the three guys behind me.
Pointing to them individually, I said, 'Joe Lampshire,
Martyn Parrish and Simon Pinchbeck . . . these guys are
either liars, and losers, or they are telling you the truth.
And if it is the truth, and it is the good news of Jesus
Christ, today, folks, it is available for you too.

'If you bow your heads with us, I will say a prayer for
you, and if you want Jesus in your life just say the prayer
with me.'

Glancing behind me at the three men, I marvelled at
how God had really changed their lives, and that we had
spent the last couple of hours telling these people about
the awesome life-changing power of God.

Some time ago, Joe, Martyn and Simon were just like
the people in the audience – lost, hurting, confused, not
knowing which way to turn – and now, here they were,
sharing their lives with others.

Looking at Joe, with his head bent and his lips silently moving in prayer, I thought of the time he first
came to a Tough Talk meeting with Arthur White, who'd
introduced him to me. I remembered Joe's boyish face,
eager to drink in all the sights and sounds of that
evening. He was a young Christian who was hungry for
direction and purpose in his Christian life.

'How much weight do you lift?' he'd asked me, eyes
sparkling, eating up all the information he could get.

Here he was now, a part of Tough Talk ministries, a British power-lifting champion, willing those who didn't know Jesus to make a commitment.

Then memories of Martyn, when he'd first walked into a Tough Talk prayer meeting soon after he came to faith, jumped into my mind. He'd looked nervous and pale and I could sense his mind churning over with thoughts like 'What am I doing here?' He'd had so many questions about God, the Bible, Jesus. It was fortunate that he worked for me and, throughout the day whenever he'd had a question, I would try and answer it as truthfully as possible. Now, people were asking *him* questions about his faith and he didn't hesitate to answer them.

And last, but not least, Simon.

I would never have thought that a towering, twenty-stone ex-policeman would be standing on the stage with me, sharing his life with total strangers and encouraging them to respond to the message of salvation.

I remembered his first Tough Talk meeting. It was in a prison and Simon was the first speaker that morning. The meeting was being held in the prison gym hall, and it seemed that most of the prisoners had turned up to hear us. I handed Simon the mike after I introduced us all and as Simon stood up and said, 'I was a police officer for twenty-three years . . . ' the hall erupted into aggressive jeering and shouting. It seemed as though a riot was going to break out at any moment. My first thought was to leg it, but Simon stood strong and kept talking. Slowly the noise abated and, after Simon finished all that he had to say, he was given a standing ovation!

The memories of these guys will always be with me as I think about how, from day to day, the Lord is continually changing them, and me.

My eyes scanned the crowd of people before me as each head was bowed, and silently I prayed that they would open their hearts to the Lord and not refuse His offer of a new life.

'Lord Jesus,' I prayed as we stood on the platform believing that there would be people responding to our stories and God's Word, 'I thank You that You died on the cross for me; that believing in You, my sins are now forgiven. I now accept you as my Lord and Saviour. Thank You, Jesus, for this new start.' The auditorium resounded to a loud 'Amen'.

The meeting was over. People flocked to talk to the guys and me and, once again, a warm feeling enveloped me as I thought about how God had touched these guys' lives. And I wondered to myself if, in the crowd of people today, there would be other men who would one day be part of Tough Talk . . .

Ian McDowall, Tough Talk

JOE
LAMPSHIRE

1

Doomed

'Shall we have a bottle of champagne, Joe?'

'All right, then, let's have a bottle of the Moët. Make it two, and stick it on the fantastic plastic,' I replied.

Mr friend – slim, smartly dressed, a real handsome bloke – caught the barman's eye, and he quickly dispensed the bottles of Moët in ice buckets.

Standing in the bar, in the middle of the City of London, surrounded by my friends and other City workers, I felt special. The atmosphere was electric, buzzing, with the latest house music pumping through speakers high on the wall. Aftershave and perfume permeated the air, making me feel dizzy with expectation.

'This is the life!' I looked around at the other young men and women, flushed with the energy of youth and with money to spend – or at least, with no limit on the company account!

Slurping greedily from my champagne glass, I eyed my friend who was cracking a joke. I wanted to respond with a hearty laugh but a thought had just popped into my head and I had to really concentrate to get rid of it.

DOOMED . . . YOU HAVE SINNED . . . YOU WILL DIE.

A shudder coursed through my body and I gripped my glass tighter. It took all my strength to focus my thoughts.

'Joe!' Another friend, Chris, tapped my arm. 'Are you all right?'

'I'm fine. I think the bubbles have gone to my head,' I lied.

Taking a cigar out of his pocket, Chris handed it to me. 'Here, take this. Twenty quid, but what's money between friends?'

I took the cigar and unwrapped it. Lighting it, I inhaled deeply. The thick, piquant smoke hit its mark and I coughed.

Chris burst out laughing. 'Bit too much for you, mate?'

My head cleared, wiping out the bad thoughts that had once again plagued me.

When would they stop?

Later, lying in bed, I willed the intoxicating feeling to obliterate my waking and, more importantly, my sleeping mind. At that moment, I wanted to be totally out of it – out of my head, out of mind, out of this world. Not dead, but far away from *me*.

Slowly, as the effects of the champagne lulled my body into a semi-conscious state, I eased my mind into blankness and slept.

DOOMED.

I couldn't move. Frozen into immobility, I felt strong, powerful hands grab me. Panic welled up; I couldn't think, speak or even open my eyes.

Effortlessly, the hands pulled me out of bed, hurtling me across the bedroom, through the door, and head first down the stairs. My mind jumped into action and I tried to battle against the forces of darkness that had so overwhelmed me. But I was no match for them. But as the front door loomed up ahead, I drew in as much oxygen as my lungs could take, and forced my eyelids to open.

The luminous numbers on the clock facing my bed read 03:00.

Breathless, panting, as sweat bubbles burst through my skin, a fear gripped me – a fear I had known since the day I had used the Ouija board.

'When will this ever end?' I thought desperately. '*When?*'

2

My Hero

'That's it. That's it! I've had enough of you. Out, out! I want you out of my life for good!'

My mum's voice echoed through my head. I had tried to block out my parents arguing by covering my ears with my hands, but I could still hear them attacking each other verbally, and it was horrible.

I wished I hadn't heard that last sentence. My mum had told my dad to leave in such a way that I knew she'd meant it. I don't know how I knew; I could just tell by the tone. The bitter feelings that had clung to those words said it all for me.

Slowly, my dad came into the kitchen, hanging his head and muttering, '. . . ignorant woman. Hasn't got a clue what a real man needs.'

Dad stopped in front of me and then he fell to his knees. It scared me, seeing him kneeling down, but I didn't move. I stared at his face. Tears began to slide down his cheeks and his nose ran. I had never seen my dad like this before. What was the matter with him?

'Dad, Dad,' I whispered.

But he didn't answer me. He clasped his hands to his face and wept all the more. I followed suit, falling to my knees and clasping my own hands to my face. I was crying too, because I knew something was drastically wrong with my dad.

Dad was my hero. He was tall – well, to me anyway – with broad shoulders, an athletic build, and a strong face. He was the life and soul of any party. Men and women loved Billy Lampshire, and Billy Lampshire loved life. Dad was the bright light in a dark place. To my young mind, he was the strongest man in the world, the toughest man in the world. He was the only person that could make me laugh out loud – I'd hold my splitting sides as he cracked joke after joke. Yet, here he was, broken and crumpled in front of me, looking to me for help.

It was hard for an eight-year-old to understand what was happening to him. Maybe he was sick. Did he need a doctor? Did he need some money? Maybe I could give him some of what I'd saved in my money box. What did he need? I felt helpless.

Wearily, Dad stood up, still muttering; he stroked my head and headed out of the door. Not a word to me – he just left. Hearing his car rev, I knew that he was going to the pub. Whenever Mum and Dad had a row, Dad would finish it off by having a drink in the pub with his mates.

Tormented by my thoughts and not knowing how to deal with them, I went into the kitchen to see Mum. She was standing at the sink, looking out of the window. Her back was straight. She wasn't moving.

'Mum?'

Turning her head slowly, she smiled at me. 'Yes, Joe?'

'Mum, can I go and play with Tim?'

She nodded. 'Yes, Joe, but be sure to be back in time for tea.'

I fled out of the house and banged on Tim's door. He conveniently lived next door. We were the same age and great friends.

Soon we were racing across the road and straight into the fields, playing tag. The wide open space of the fields transported me far, far away from the turmoil that was my home. I ran and ran and ran with Tim chasing me, dodging him as he stretched out his hand to catch me. He could never catch me. I was too fast for him.

Breathlessly, we finally lay on our backs with the grass tickling our ears. The sky above was vast, endless. It was amazing, watching the clouds gently move along as though pulled by an invisible thread. The sun shone brightly high up in the sky.

'There's so much up there in the sky and it's so far away,' I thought to myself. It made me seem so small as I looked up. I wondered if Granddad could see me down here. I knew that he had died and was now in heaven, and heaven was up in the sky somewhere. I believed it, too, because the sky was so big.

An incredible feeling of peace crept over me, and I felt like sleeping for a long time.

Then Tim nudged me. 'Joe, we'd better be getting back or our mums will punish us.' He didn't have to tell me twice. My mum had caught me swearing once and had taken me into the kitchen and washed my mouth out with soap. The memory was painful and I ran fast to get home in time.

'Tim, shall we go on the swings?'

'OK, Joe. Let's have something to eat first of all, then I'll knock for you.'

Walking home from school with Tim was a two-minute affair. The school was just at the bottom of my road and it was safe for my friend and me to go together.

Searching my pockets for my door key, I couldn't find it. I knew that Mum would be angry with me so I carefully slid my skinny arm through the letter box, stretching it as far as it could go. Bingo! I clutched the short lever and the door opened with my arm still stuck in the slot. Quickly, I pulled it out, and went inside. Then I heard my mum's voice.

'Joe! Get in the car. We're going.'

I frowned. 'Going where?'

Mum said, 'Just get in the car.'

Turning to go out of the door, I noticed something was missing. Some of the pictures that had been on the wall of George, my elder brother, and me, were gone. I slowly walked to Mum's car.

'Hurry up, slowcoach.' George was coming up behind me, followed by Mum.

As Mum pulled out of our cul-de-sac, I had a funny feeling that I would not be living in that house again.

'Mum, where are we going?'

'Your dad and I have decided that because we can't seem to live together it's best, especially for you boys, that we live apart,' she replied.

So my feelings had been bang on target!

George looked out the window as the familiar streets passed us by.

'When will we see Dad again?' I asked.

'When he can be bothered to drag himself from the pub, or maybe when he's had enough of football and remembers he has two children . . . *That's* when you'll see him again, Joe.'

I leaned back against the seat, feeling very upset. What was Mum talking about? Dad would want to see us every day! How could he *not* want to see us? My mind did a few somersaults.

'Maybe Dad wants to see George and not me.'

I suddenly remembered getting lost at his local football ground. Dad had been livid and I'd thought he was going to shake the living daylights out of me when I'd turned up as though nothing was wrong. There were countless other occasions when I'd messed up and Dad would end up shouting or swearing at me. He'd constantly gritted his teeth at me, usually over some trouble I'd got myself into.

That was the reason Dad didn't want us – or rather, me – around him any more! I tried to hold back the tears that were just on the edge, ready to spill down my face. My dad had had enough of *me!*

3

Family Trouble

'This is Steve.'

I was deeply engrossed in watching my favourite cartoon characters on TV when Mum came into the room and made her announcement. I glanced up and saw behind her, overshadowing her, the tallest man I had ever seen.

'Wow,' I mouthed.

He was the original Jack and the Beanstalk giant. He was huge. He filled the whole door frame, overlapping at the edges.

'Hi, Joe.' His voice seemed to start somewhere deep inside him. He held out his hand and I shook it. My small hand got swallowed up in his huge paw, and I thought to myself, 'If he ever gives me a wallop, I'll be dead!'

I carried on watching TV as Mum and Steve went into the kitchen.

'Who *is* that man?' I wondered. 'Why has Mum brought him home?'

For the past few months we'd been living at my nan's – my mum's Mum. She was a bit like a character out of a Dickens novel, very Victorian, very prim and proper,

and she expected children, especially little boys, to be
seen and not heard. It was a bit of a nightmare living in
her house. I couldn't shout, or run up and down the
stairs. I couldn't speak with food in my mouth. She
would even look behind my ears to see if I had washed
them properly. In fact, though I loved her dearly, I much
preferred living with Mum and Dad and George, visiting Nan for a few hours – and then going home.

George and I had always shared a bedroom. We were
very close as brothers, even though there were four
years between us. We understood each other and
enjoyed each other's company. But now that we lived in
Buckhurst Hill with Nan, things between George and I
had changed, and I found it troubling.

'First my dad doesn't want to live with us because of
me, and now my brother doesn't want to have much to
do with me either!'

It wasn't nice to think that there was something that
was causing people to back away from me. My brother
and I were growing apart moment by moment, and it
was upsetting. I didn't understand it, so I'd try to find
ways to wind him up.

Mum and Nan were working at the insurance company Mum owned. So, most evenings after school, it was
just George and me at home. Pushing open his bedroom
door I would open my mouth to say something, but
George wouldn't give me a chance.

'Get out! I don't want you in here.'

'Why?'

'Just get out,' he'd snap.

'All right.' Closing the door softly behind me, I slipped
the key into the lock and turned it. Leaning against the
door I called out, 'George! Come here a minute.'

He ignored me, but I went on and on. Finally I could
see the door knob turning – and then he exploded.

'Let me out, let me out!'

He banged on the door, and rattled the knob. I held my sides as I doubled over in hysterics.

George had had enough, and so had Mum. So, I found myself having to make my way straight from school to Mum's offices in Loughton. I loved it! I loved going on the bus on my own; it made me feel so grown up.

One gloomy afternoon, I was waiting for the bus. It seemed to be taking ages. I thought, 'I could've walked quicker.' I had a lot of unspent energy and, as I looked up at the bus shelter, it was as though I knew what to do. I clambered on top and was soon doing an imperson- ation of Gene Kelly in *Singing in the Rain*. My mates were rolling up with laughter as I pranced around. Nan's neighbour saw me and told me to come down. I took no notice of her. She was quick to report my antics to my mum who, at first, wouldn't believe that I could do such a thing. But I finally had to admit it. I hated getting into trouble, but whenever a 'good' idea came into my head, I just felt it was natural for me to follow it through. And I did, which usually got me into trouble.

Dad would collect George and me fortnightly on a Friday and take us back to our old house to spend the weekend with him. I loved being with my dad. He had still managed to maintain his hero status in my eyes, no matter what was going on between him and Mum.

It was wonderful to meet up with Tim and my old buddies. We would roam around the streets, sniffing out trouble, irritating adults and causing havoc; we'd climb garden walls and trespass into neighbouring gardens, driving people mad. But my brother was becoming more and more introverted. He was so closed up inside himself that no one could even guess what he was think- ing; he gave nothing away. The months raced by, and now, whenever Dad came to pick us up, George would refuse to go. He wouldn't even leave Nan's house to tell my dad he wasn't going, he would just stay inside his bedroom, lost in his own world. I could sense that George had lost the adoration he once had for Dad, and was just not interested. Still, I was glad to have Dad all to myself. It had been niggling me for some time to ask Dad why he left me.

'I never left, son. It's your mother who left me and took my two boys with her.'

It sounded great, but something was not adding up. Even I, young as I was, knew that families fell apart for a reason; it didn't just happen. So why did mine? I brushed aside the vicious rows and confrontations that had regularly happened between Mum and Dad. I 'forgot' the times Dad had come home reeking of alcohol, flushed in the face, ready to launch into battle with Mum. I just wanted to know why we now had to live apart.

My dad had been a professional footballer with Leyton Orient for a very short time. Anyone who knew him knew that that was his first love and I don't think he ever really lost it. He'd worked for the BBC for a number of years as a stagehand, setting up scenery for television shows. Now, though, he was a bricklayer, running his own firm.

Dad wasn't too quick to spend money on George or me, but when he did, he was generous. One weekend, he took me to Ilford to buy me a pair of Puma trainers. They were all the rage and I lovingly put them on and walked up and down the shop, looking in the mirror. I felt on top of the world.

'C'mon son, let's get your old Dad a whistle.' He glanced down at me, and then at his friend Alf, who'd accompanied us on this shopping trip. We went looking for a two-piece suit (that's what Dad meant when he said whistle – cockney rhyming slang, 'whistle and flute', suit!).

Dad and I were really getting on well. I was happy with my new trainers and Dad seemed to be in a very good mood. Then, it all changed. We entered a shop and, after Dad had picked out the best suit in the place and tried it on, we all stood at the counter as he handed over his card.

We waited for what seemed ages, then Dad said, ''Ere, Alf, take him out for an ice cream.' A look passed between them that made me wonder what was going on.

As we stepped over the threshold of the shop, Dad shot past Alf and me, faster than Roadrunner. What was even more alarming, the shop assistant flew after him, followed by a whole group of people, all chasing Dad.

'Dad! Dad, wait!' I screamed, tearing away from Alf and charging after the last person who was running after my dad. It wasn't long before I lost sight of them. I turned every which way to see if I could see Dad, but it was futile. Then, as I looked about, I realised that I was now lost myself. I was frightened and wanted to cry. Who could I ask for help? Where was the nearest police-man? Suddenly, I was yanked by the scruff of my neck, almost dangling on my toes.

'C'mon Joe, let's get out of here,' said Alf.

'But I want my dad, I . . . '

'That's enough, let's go.'

Alf took me back to where Dad had parked his car. There was Dad, bold as brass, sitting on the bonnet! He looked at his watch and said, 'Took your time. C'mon let's go.'

I wanted to know what had happened to make Dad leave the shop in such a hurry; why had he been chased

by all those people? But I sensed from the vibes that
were passing between Alf and Dad that now was not the
time for asking questions.

Within a few months my dad had left the shores of
England for the delights of California. It would be four
years before I saw him again.

Secretly, I'd hoped that my parents would make up and
we would all live under one roof again. It was a regular
dream that I would have: Mum, Dad, George and me,
living in our old house in Loughton by the fields, just
getting on with each other – no rows or violent outbursts, Dad not going to the pub so often, George and
me back close again . . . But my dream never came true.
Steve seemed to be spending more and more time at our
house. He was nearly a permanent fixture. I wanted to
hate him, but I didn't. In fact, he was a nice bloke and a
positive, stabilising influence in my life, and I started to
become quite attached to him. And, for all my dreaming,
it was no real surprise to me when Steve and Mum got
married.

Nanny Goose was Dad's mother. Her real name was
Marie but she got the name Nanny Goose because she
had a goose as a pet in her garden and the name stuck.
Now that Dad had gone to live in America, he would
phone me occasionally, but it wasn't enough. So I would
go and visit Nanny Goose and she would keep me up to
date about him.

I loved going to her house. She lived alone, as my
granddad had died before I was born, and she seemed to
welcome my company. She had endless stories to tell me
about my dad and his brothers and the things they got
up to when they were much younger. She would tell me
about her life too, especially with Granddad. She also

told me how she would meet up with her friends and hold séances; one of her friends was a 'medium' who would lead them through a procedure in which they would try to contact their deceased loved ones. It was fascinating.

I loved to hear her stories, whatever they were about. I never once thought I would be having 'supernatural' stories of my own.

4

Life After Death

I missed my dad. Since he had emigrated, he hardly wrote and, when he did, I would devour each letter from beginning to end. Dad's letters were the highlight of my life. For an eleven-year-old, to get a letter with an American stamp on was mind-blowing. Dad would also put some money inside, green and white dollar bills, to be pored over along with the letter. I would rub my hands over the sheets and smell them, just to get a hint of my dad's flavour. I would re-read the letters constantly until I knew them word for word. George was more conservative. He would read them once and that was it. I, though, wanted more; my dad would write that he loved and missed me. But, I thought, if that was so, why then did he leave me? Deep down I knew that he and mum had rowed and argued a lot, but why had that meant that he'd had to leave *me*? It wasn't as though he had moved a few streets away or perhaps even to Scotland. He'd gone to live thousands and thousands of miles away. In my mind at the time, you put a great distance between yourself and the person you didn't like . . . But I held onto his letters – my one tangible link with him.

Mum's relationship with Steve was so different from her relationship with Dad. They really got on well together; they were always holding hands. Mum was clearly a lot happier and content with her life and our household was peaceful. Nan had handed the house over to Steve and Mum, and she had moved out to a lovely flat round the corner. It was nice not to have Nan's Victorian ways cramping my style, her eyes everywhere, knowing what I was up to.

School was not so good. I was now attending Buckhurst Hill County High School for Boys. I loved all the physical education lessons – and that was it. I had absolutely no interest in any other subject; it was all a waste of time as far as I was concerned. I wasn't alone in thinking this. A lot of the other boys were of the same frame of mind. It got so bad that the history teacher couldn't stand the stress and strain of our bad behaviour, so would wheel in the television and let us watch *Neighbours* for the duration of the lesson. And in science, we were unteachable. My class were well known throughout the school as being disruptive. Any class would know we were in the classroom above them because we would snatch bags from under chairs and lob them out of the window, one after the other. No teacher was safe. We'd place drawing pins on their chairs and howl with laughter when they jumped up rubbing their bottoms! Smashing windows was another favourite pastime, and hurling two pence pieces at the window, causing slot marks in the glass. Fighting was a daily occurrence.

I don't know why I didn't want to learn; being in a class full of unruly boys who were of the same mindset as me did not help. But underlying my bad behaviour was a silent rage. At the time, I didn't identify it as a rage, a sort of misplaced anger, but it was there all the same. There was no one on earth I could share it with. It would rear up in me; and, at school, I could indulge in all types or errant behaviour and get away with it. I was always plotting and planning what I could do next.

As each year passed by, I got worse. There was a forest area attached to the school where no first-year pupil was allowed to go. My friends and I would lie in wait, up in the trees, waiting for disobedient boys who were tempted to spend their lunchtime in a natural setting. Once they were under our tree, we would pounce on them, quickly tie them to the trunk with their own tie and mercilessly whip them with stinging nettles. They would cry and scream, but we were deaf to their pleading; and I'd get a sense of power over the younger kids that would appease my own feelings of loss and helplessness.

My lack of real contact with Dad was continuing to be hard to bear. I couldn't talk it over with George. He would just shrug and say something like, 'It's life.' And I didn't feel comfortable bringing up the subject of Dad with my mum, as she would dismiss it: 'Joe, your dad left you. He has the problem.' And I could feel the web of confusion in my heart and mind getting more and more tangled up.

I was very interested in death, and used to wonder why we humans were here. I used to think, 'Why am *I* here?' I remember being in the bathroom once, thinking about dying. Panic began to well up in me and my heart began to pump twice as fast. 'What happens when someone dies? Where do they go? When's Mum going to die? When am I going to die?' I couldn't bear to think about not ever having my mum around. And what about my dad? What if he died? He lived so far away I was finding it hard trying to remember his smile, the sound of his voice – if he died, would I be able to hold on to my memories of him?

I asked George about this. After all, he was older than me. He might know more about the process of death.

'When you die, you die. It's something that happens to every single person, you live your life, then you drop dead. People come to your funeral, bring flowers, cry, and then after a while, they forget you and die themselves. That's it. *Finito.*'

This made me feel worse. Still, I reasoned that I was young and had at least fifty or more years left until I had to worry about leaving this earth for good. But – death seemed so final!

I loved ghost stories, in fact anything spooky, such as UFOs and scary movies. Anything to do with the paranormal would grab my attention. I wanted to know if there was another world somewhere 'out there'. Were there other kinds of species apart from humans who had the same sort of intelligence, or were cleverer than us? Did we leave this life and begin another life elsewhere? I wanted – in fact, *needed* – to know.

It was Nanny Goose and my uncle Harry who really opened up my mind to the possibility of life after death.

'Granddad had been dead for a few years, and I was still feeling so lonely,' said Nanny Goose. 'I didn't know if he was all right. So when my friend the medium said that she would get in touch with him, I was all for it.'

Sitting in the front room whilst Nanny Goose was telling her story was very spooky; I even hoped that Granddad would put in an appearance so that I could get a 'feel' of who he was.

'Sitting round the little square coffee table, my friend told us to place our hands on the top, which we did, and she began to summon the spirit of your granddad . . .'

Uncle Harry, who was a little boy at the time of this séance, went on, 'She said, "Are you Lenny Lampshire? If so, rock three times," and then the table moved from side to side three times, from leg to leg. I wanted to run out of the room.'

But what really terrified him was when the medium asked the spirit, 'Lenny Lampshire, find your youngest son in this room.' The table began to rock violently, everyone took their hands off it except for the medium – 'And then it walked towards me,' said Uncle Harry. 'I was petrified. I couldn't move.'

Even as he told me, it seemed as though Uncle Harry was reliving the horror. I couldn't believe what I was hearing. It made me wonder if there really was life after death. Judging by that story, I supposed there must be; I knew that Nanny Goose would not lie about it.

I was determined to see Dad. It wasn't right that we were living so far apart; anything could happen to him . . .

I asked my mum if I could go and see him.

'Joe, it's up to your father if he wants to see you. He knows where you live, so if he sends the money for your fare, of course you can go.'

That set me off furiously writing to Dad, begging him to send money so that George and I could visit him. It took some time for Dad to respond, and my behaviour got worse. I had a kind of 'don't care' attitude that affected everything I did. I had a crush on the daughter of one of my stepdad's friends, and it was during an outing to a safari park that I sort of lost my head. She and I were in a pedal boat in the middle of the lake. A duck with her ducklings were near our boat and this girl said, 'Ohh, aren't they sweet!' I wondered why she was paying stupid ducklings such a lovely compliment. She hadn't said anything like that to me. I casually stretched out my hand, caught one of the ducklings and held it under the water for a while. Its kicks got less and less, until they stopped. Then I let go. I had no feeling about what I had just done. I didn't even look back. I carried on pedalling.

Finally, one day I came home from school and my mum thrust a letter into my hand. It was from Dad. He had sent the air fare for Nanny Goose, George and I. My head felt as though it would burst with the multiple thoughts that were jumbled up in my mind. I made a calendar and I would cross off each day until it was time to leave. I was so happy. I would think about how Dad would react when he first saw us. Then I would think about how happy he would be to have his sons so close to him – which would lead me into daydreams about how he would be so sad to see us go back to England that he would come with us.

San Diego was breathtaking. It was everything I could possibly have dreamed of and more. The weather was constantly warm. My dad's apartment, a condo, was like a holiday home. The swimming pool was far better than the local baths at home. It was surrounded by palm trees and the beach was only a stone's throw away. It was the closest thing to heaven for me.

The three weeks we spent with Dad were great. He rarely got irritated with me like he used to do when I was younger. He seemed a lot happier.

At the airport, both George and I were plunged into depression. Dad could only come so far to see us off. He wasn't allowed to go through to the departure lounge. I walked through the tunnel and at the furthest point I turned to look at Dad, tears streaming down my face. He waved; he was crying, too. I stood and looked at him, my eyes searching every contour of his face to imprint it in my mind. Why did it have to be this way? Why couldn't

Dad live in England? Better still, why couldn't we live in San Diego? But Dad never asked us to stay, nor mentioned that he wanted to come back to England.

The first few weeks after our holiday, I was still buzzing with all things American: 'In the States they do this. In San Diego they do that.' My speech was peppered with Americanisms. But, as the weeks wore on, a realisation that Dad was *there* and I was *here* seeped in and brought my mood back down to earth.

Some of my friends had developed an interest in the paranormal. During a geography field trip, they made their own Ouija board. One evening, whilst the teachers were chilling out, we gathered in a bedroom and began to use the board. I felt a bit uncomfortable with it because I knew, from Nanny Goose's stories, that the 'power' behind Ouija was real.

I stood on the outskirts of the group of boys who were around the table, and the glass began to move. I left. Even though I was interested in such things, I just wasn't ready to get involved with spirits. I lay on my bed questioning myself.

'You're a chicken, Joe. Get up and go into that room. You're a baby. Nothing's gonna happen to you, just go.'

But I couldn't bring myself to deal with the potential outcome.

Not just yet.

5

Future Promise?

'George, turn the telly up.'

George pointed the remote control at the screen and the volume increased. I was sprawled across the settee and George was sitting on the floor with his back against the armchair.

The incidental music blared out as the characters on screen enacted their roles. The film was *A Nightmare on Elm Street* with Freddy Krueger as the evil killer of children. I had seen the film many times before, but it never ceased to frighten me. Freddy's burnt and scarred face, and the knives that he had for fingers were especially chilling. Clutching the cushion tight, I watched with morbid fascination as the children were pursued by their wicked enemy.

That same night, as always, my dreams would be some kind of re-enactment of the film. I would fight sleep as I didn't want to dream, but my eyelids would grow heavy and I would drift off into a place like Elm Street to be chased by my own demons.

A Nightmare on Elm Street was one of my favourite films and I never tired of watching it. *Poltergeist* and *The Exorcist* and films like that really intrigued me. I loved the way my heart would thump at twice its normal rate. My stomach would contract and shivers ran up and down my spine. Were the dead walking around on another planet? Could they see us? Could they help us? I wanted answers.

I had known Emma for a short while. We were both Sea Cadets and instantly became friends. I loved the way she would stand up for herself and speak her mind. Her bad behaviour had an effect on me and I would play up too. Emma lived in Loughton, not too far from Nanny Goose. She was an attractive girl and full of life. So, being bold, I asked her out – to see the latest horror movie.

I went to her house a good hour before the programme started. I rang the bell and her mum opened the door.

'Are you playing Solitaire?' I asked. Emma's mum had a pack of playing cards placed before her on the coffee table.

'No. These are tarot cards. They predict your future.'

'Really?' All thoughts of going to the cinema fled from my mind. I wanted her, right there and then, to tell me about my future life. But how could I ask her?

'Sit down, love.'

Obediently I sat opposite her in an armchair. She shuffled the cards in her hand and placed some on the table.

'Do you want your future told?'

'Yeah, I do.' Excitement, coupled with an eerie expectancy, rippled through my body and mind. On the one hand, I really wanted to know, yet there was a voice in my head saying, 'You shouldn't be doing this.' I ignored the voice of caution and told her to go ahead. I wanted her to tell me that I would become rich and famous – but she didn't.

By the time Emma had got herself ready, her mum still hadn't told me anything that would cause me to believe that I was going to have a great life. Still, I was glad she hadn't told me anything bad.

Later that night, alone in my bed, I wondered about Emma's mum. How was she able to know about the future and what was going to happen? Did she possess special powers? If so, how did you get these special powers? And, more importantly, could *I* have these powers? Where did I get them from? I lay awake for a while, churning these thoughts over and over and over. Remembering scenes from the film I'd just watched, I thought about 'spirit guides'. Could I conjure up spirits? I wondered if anyone could do it. What did I have to say?

Sitting up in bed, I turned the bedside lamp on. I closed my eyes. I had read somewhere that if you really wanted something to happen you had to keep saying and believing it and it would happen. Tentatively, I opened my eyes, half-expecting to see some kind of apparition standing in the middle of my room.

Nothing.

School held no great hopes for me and, even though I had taken six exams, I knew that the only As I'd be getting would be for being 'Absent'. But Steve was able to get me a part-time position as a clerk in the building society where he worked. It was fantastic. Here I was, supposedly doing revision, and I was being offered a job! The pay was huge – well, for a sixteen-year-old it was good money. I felt special with money to spend; I felt good. Most of my school friends had Saturday jobs or no job at all and were still dependent on their parents. But I was my own man, able to make my own decisions about what I did with my hard-earned cash.

Unfortunately, it didn't last long. The bubble burst when Steve left the building society. The new manager

called me into her office and told me they wouldn't need
me after that day. When I went home and told Steve, he
said, 'I'm sorry. I should have thought that when I left they
might want you to leave as well. I feel really bad about it.'

'Nah, don't worry, it's not your fault,' I said.

But the truth was I was gutted, and yes, in a way it
was my stepdad's fault. If he had still been working
there, so would I. But I knew I couldn't dwell on the negative so I set about trying to find myself a proper job –
one that I could get on my own merits.

'So you feel that you will get As in all your exams?'

I nodded, confidently. 'Yes, I am expected to do really
well,' I lied.

'What are your hobbies?' asked the interviewer.

I spied a Charlton Athletic badge on his desk. 'Well, I
used to play football for the England youth team . . . '

'Really? That's marvellous!' he beamed.

I knew what he was thinking: 'He's a straight A stu-
dent; he can play for our company's football team.'

'Thanks for coming, Joe. We will be in touch with you
shortly.'

As soon as I got home, the interviewer's secretary had
called me. She asked me when I could start. I wasted no
time in telling her, 'Straight away.'

I was well chuffed and a bit nervous, thinking, 'What
have I got myself into?' but both my mum and Steve
assured me that I would be fine. And I was. I could do no
wrong with my new boss. My confidence in my abilities
grew. Nothing seemed impossible for me. I was so full of
myself, blagging my first proper job, that I felt invincible;
able to do whatever I put my mind to. Most evenings
after work I was in a bar, drinking and smoking cigars. I
was a sharp dresser and took pride in my appearance.
Emma was history as I made the acquaintance of other

young women. I felt that I could climb any mountain and succeed in all I did.

Six years passed really quickly (it does when you're having fun!). I had a great time, and I managed to do some work too . . . Eventually I was headhunted and became a manager in a senior post – which meant more money. I loved the job. My office was open-plan, and so was my time. At the interview I was told: 'You can do what you like, when you like, but you must get your work done. Then we'll all be happy.'

It was like a dream. I would work like a slave for as long as it took to get my quota of work done, and after that it was 'party-time'.

'Disco, we out tonight?'

'Disco' turned and looked at me. ''Course, Magic, meet you in the club at six.'

I gave him a thumb's up and a wink. My heart thudded with anticipation at the night ahead. The thought alone was intoxicating. I was lucky to be alive, lucky to have the money and opportunities to do anything I wanted to do. My selfish, youthful desires were being fulfilled as and when I wanted them. I had no thought of the future. I *was* the future.

The club was packed with pretty young things (including me). The smoky atmosphere, alcohol and fresh body smells was heaven to me. We soon headed for another place where most of the people who worked in the Square Mile hung out. Everyone had money to burn. It was exhilarating. Music blaring, bodies shimmering, pressing closer to each other . . . It wasn't hard to find a female who oozed lust and willingness, and who found me appealing.

Disco and I would woo a few ladies back to my office. I had a twenty-four hour pass and it was just a matter of walking through. In my office, I would play some CDs to get us into the mood. Out would come the wine and spirits from my governor's office, we'd raid the fridge in the kitchen and have ourselves a party.

'This is the life,' I thought, 'my life!'

The future was looking good and I believed I knew how the course of my life would go. I was set. Or so I thought.

The forest whizzed past me as the motorbike roared through the country lanes. It was midnight on a Saturday and I had just spent the last few hours catching up with my friend Nick. I had known him for years. He didn't work in the city like me; he worked in Harlow, Essex as a shop assistant. His life was far removed from mine, but whenever I met up with him, we would just pick up from where we left off.

The air was cool as I gathered speed, twisting and turning along the road. The thought popped into my head – 'To be young is the best thing ever.'

Nick and I had arranged to meet at his brother's house. When I arrived, the smell of marijuana was thick in the air. Nick's brother handed me a joint and I inhaled deeply as I followed him through to the living room.

'Hello, mate,' said Nick. He had a fat joint in his hand and I knew he was stoned.

'I see you're all right, Nick.'

He grinned.

I didn't smoke 'puff' a lot, but when I did, it was enjoyable. It mellowed me out and enabled me to think deeply about subjects that I probably wouldn't even have considered if I was in my right state of mind.

Nick, his brother Ray and Ray's wife were into the Ouija board. They didn't use it every day – in fact they didn't get it out every time I visited them. But whenever we'd had a few joints and some deep inhalations from the 'bong pipe' (a device used for smoking cannabis), and a couple of cans of lager, I just knew that one of the three would suggest, 'Shall we get the Ouija out?'

This night, the lights were dimmed and we gathered around the coffee table, and I began to feel small waves of excitement. Usually, I just took it as a laugh, something that I got involved with whenever I visited Ray's house. But, this particular night I wasn't feeling quite myself.

The air was thick with expectation. We were waiting for the spirits to come. And they always would come – every time I was there, the spirits would make themselves known after we used a certain chant. Except this time.

For about ten, fifteen minutes, an eerie silence enveloped the room. Impatience was growing in me – I wanted something to happen. Ray got his snake out of the vivarium. It was a brown reticulated python, cold and smooth to the touch. Ray loved his snake. He said holding it helped him to concentrate. Ray hung the snake around his neck; it slithered slowly through his hands and its head reared up as though tasting the air.

I *really* wanted something to happen, but I knew I couldn't manufacture spirits. We would just have to try chanting again. Ray put the snake back. I could feel the mounting tension as we tried to focus on calling up the spirits. I felt desperate to have an encounter with some spirits; good or bad, I didn't care. I wanted some action.

Then the glass began to move.

My first thought was: 'Who's pushing it?' I took a sneaky look around and I could see that everyone was only lightly touching the glass. This thing was for real. The glass slid backwards and forwards – 6,6,6,6,6,6 – at such an accelerated rate, none of us could have done it. It was a spirit. I felt freaked by what was happening and wanted to leave, but somehow I was compelled to stay and see it through. I asked it to tell me where my dad lived and the glass moved again, spelling out CALIFORNIA. Then the glass went back to the number six, again repeating the number very fast. My mouth was dry. The others were silent, stealing glances at me. Because I had taken the lead I continued to ask the questions. Then, off its own initiative, the glass spelt

DOOM.

I caught my breath. I tried to swallow. 'Who?'

JOE.

I tried to put on a brave face to the others but inside I was petrified. Why had this spirit picked me out? It couldn't have been my granddad or any dead family member – I felt hostility emanating from the glass.

YOU WILL DIE.

'Who?' I whispered.

YOU.

I took a deep breath. I wanted to jump up and run out of the house but I knew that that was not the way you left the Ouija board. I wanted to ask Ray to take over the questioning but no one was saying a word. It was left to me. I asked it, 'How am I going to die?'

MOTORBIKE.

An overwhelming feeling of weakness came over me and I really wanted to stop. I was disturbed that the spirit was honing in on me. I tried to change the subject.

'Is Elvis still alive?'

YOU HAVE SINNED.

By now I was sweating and the effort it was taking for me to answer the spirit was draining me of all my strength. I was really, really scared. Playing the Ouija board was just for a laugh; I had done it many times before, and whenever we had had a spiritual response, once it was over, that was it. But this was something way, way out of my experience and it wasn't funny.

The snake began to get overactive in the vivarium. Normally, being cold-blooded, it took its time to slither around. Not tonight. It moved at a quicker pace. I wondered if it, too, was being affected by the spirit.

I wanted the spirit to go and leave me alone. In the back of my mind I knew that I had to leave soon as I had to get some sleep to enable me to face work the next day; I just wanted to relax, yet here I was, stuck in a room with a spirit or spirits that had very strong malevolent intentions towards me. *Why?*

The spirit dragged me through two hours of mental and spiritual torture. Every fibre of my being wanted out, but it was as though an invisible force had bound me and the others to the board and had no intentions of letting us go. The others were feeling the bad vibes too and wanted to stop.

'It's time we called it a day now, don't you think?' said one of them.

We all agreed. But the spirit didn't seem to respond to the others' voices. Only mine!

I said to the spirit, 'We have to go now.'

DOOMED.

I wanted to run away, but I felt as though I had to make sure that the spirit left of its own accord. So I had to stay till it went. After a few attempts in trying to get the spirit to leave, I finally said, 'We have to go now. We will contact you tomorrow.' I had absolutely no intention of contacting this spirit or any other again, and would have said *anything* in order to get free from this bondage.

The glass moved to Goodbye and I quickly upended it and leaned back in my chair. My mind felt as though it was spinning, leaping all over the place. The night's happenings were so far out of my experience it was difficult for me to get my head together. Nick and Ray's wife were equally freaked out by the whole session and Ray said to me, 'I'm really sorry that the spirit seemed to have it in for you tonight.'

I faked a grin and said, 'No worries.'

The truth was that riding my bike home, I was worried. I was especially careful as I rode through the dark country road that went through Epping Forest. There wasn't a soul about, yet I 'sensed' that I wasn't alone.

YOU WILL DIE . . . MOTORBIKE . . .

I began to mumble the Lord's Prayer. I had learnt it at school and the words somehow made me feel stronger.

'God, Jesus, I need you now, help me to get home safely, help me.'

Thankfully I pulled up outside my home in one piece. Entering the house I know I looked normal to Mum and Steve, but I felt different inside. I was just about to climb the stairs to my room, when I noticed the family Bible. It was a huge book that had been handed down from generation to generation. I lifted it up and carried it to my room.

Lying in bed, I found it hard to sleep. I couldn't get the memory of the night's events out of my mind. Why did the spirit say I was doomed? I hadn't done anything bad to anyone. Why was it picking on me? I tossed and turned and knew that sleep was not coming. I picked up the old Bible and placed it on my chest. If the spirit decided to return, I felt that the Bible would protect me.

I was soon asleep. The morning came quickly and I went off to work.

Over the next few months, I continued my hedonistic lifestyle. I had made up my mind that I would never again play the Ouija board. And I didn't. As far as I was concerned, I was finished with the spirit world.

But it wasn't finished with me. It had only just started.

6

Attacked!

The early morning sun streamed through the slightly open curtains in my room. I had been out drinking the night before. I had been given the day off as it was Good Friday – in fact, in the City of London, everyone was off work; it was a nice break.

'Joe, would you like to come to church this morning?' Mum called up the stairs.

'Is she joking? Church!'

Mum and Steve had recently begun to attend church on a regular basis and to say that they were eager to go was an understatement. Now, they wanted to drag me along with them – on a *Saturday* morning!

'No, thanks, Mum,' I called. 'You have a good time.'

I rolled over on my side and snuggled up to my pillow. Then a voice said: 'Joe, get up and go.'

I looked around my room. Nobody there. I shook my head and thought, 'Must be my mind playing tricks on me.' I got comfortable in my bed again.

'Joe, get up and go.'

I sat up quickly. I definitely knew that I had heard a voice speaking to me, telling me to go to church. But who was it?

Joe winning the squat lift at the 2005 British
Championships with a 310 kg lift.

Joe demonstrating the squat lift at a Tough Talk street
outreach in front of Ilford Town Hall.

Joe with Dad and George.

Mr and Mrs Lampshire.

Martyn as a stock car racer.

Martyn at a Tough Talk meeting.

Martyn being baptised with his wife.

Martyn as he is now.

I called out, 'Mum, I'm coming.'

I was ready in a few seconds. Mum and Steve were waiting for me at the bottom of the stairs, hardly able to hide their surprise.

'Are we ready, then?' I said.

Mum smiled, and we all left the house.

I had been in St John's Church many times. It was just across the road from where I lived, and was attached to my old school. The school regularly used the church as part of school activities. But this time, when I entered the church, I felt as though I was seeing it for the first time. The colours of the stained-glass windows seemed more vivid. The flowers in the vases were vibrant and stunning. I felt as though I was walking into a wonderland. An incredible warm, loving feeling came over me.

A man with a baseball cap came up and introduced himself as John. I told him who I was and he said he knew my parents.

'Do you come here much?' I asked him.

'Yes. Yes, I do,' he said, smiling. 'What do you do for a living, then?'

I told him I worked in the City. Then I said, 'What work do you do?'

He smiled again. 'I'm the vicar of this church.'

I was shocked. He looked normal, like any other bloke, and yet he was the vicar!

I began to unload the experience that I'd had with the Ouija board. I hadn't told anyone about it before and I suppose that because I had kept it all inside, when the opportunity came to tell someone, I let them have it all. Nothing strange had happened to me since that night, but I still felt fear lurking inside.

John listened to me patiently, and then he said, 'Have you a Bible at home?'

'Yes,' I nodded.

'OK. Go home and read some of the Gospels, and then get back to me and we can have a chat about it.'

I smiled and said that would be great.

I pored over the Gospels – Matthew, Mark, Luke and John, telling the story of Jesus – and, as soon as I'd finished, I called John. We met often and he was the only person I felt I could be truthful with. I could really tell him what was on my mind. He inspired my interest in the Bible and became a good friend. He never seemed to get fed up with my many questions, and he seemed genuinely interested in my life.

Then I began to have disturbed dreams, nightmares about demons, hideous in appearance, physically attacking me, dragging me out of bed. I felt as though the demons were trying to suffocate and choke the life out of me. The nightly attacks intensified and became so bad that I didn't want to go to sleep at all. A few nights during the week, I would be woken up at exactly 3 a.m. No matter how deeply I was sleeping, it was as though an inner alarm was programmed for that time and I woke up. My work was being affected as my sleep was so disturbed. The threatening thoughts were always there, plaguing me . . . even when I was out with my friends, drinking champagne, trying to enjoy myself. I knew that I couldn't go and see my GP as he would put me on tablets – or perhaps suggest I saw a psychologist.

My cousin Tom had arranged to spend one particular weekend with me. We were as close as cousins could be; in fact, he was more like a brother. We had been out drinking, and Tom fell asleep as soon as his head hit the pillow. As usual, I tossed and turned and then decided to go downstairs. Steve was just turning the television off, but I told him I would probably watch a late-night movie.

'OK, I'm off to bed now,' he said, and left me alone.

I sprawled across the settee, one arm draped over the back. Exhausted, I began to drift off to sleep. Then, although I was only semi-conscious, I felt something pressing me down into the settee. I tried to resist, to sit up – I couldn't. A 'presence' that seemed tangibly evil hovered over my body, holding me down. I wanted to cry out for help – again, I couldn't. I was unable to move, talk or even think. This 'thing' had rendered me totally immobile.

I heard high-pitched laughter as a vice-like grip took hold of my left arm and proceeded to slowly drag me off the settee. I was fully awake by now, but I couldn't resist the invisible, powerful hands that held me prisoner. My mind was numb, my lips were stuck together, I couldn't even speak. I was terrified – in fact, words cannot describe how I was feeling. DOOM . . . YOU ARE GOING TO DIE . . . was this happening right now?

I tried to remember the Lord's Prayer, but I couldn't. I began to call out 'Jesus, Jesus, Jesus' in my mind, as some 'force' was keeping my mouth shut. Then, somehow, I was able to move my jaw and make the name of Jesus with my lips. I was struck with terror, but felt that I had to say this name. So I worked on saying it over and over and over again. As I kept continually saying 'Jesus', eventually the 'force' let me go, and at that point I shot up the stairs. My heart was racing – I thought I was going to have a heart attack.

Upstairs, everyone was fast asleep. I couldn't wake anyone as I knew they would say I was mad. Tom was sleeping like a baby. I was alone, shaking and fearful. I picked up my Bible and began to read it. Sweat was rolling off my body, like rain down a window pane. I flicked the pages of the Bible, looking for help. The words were all jumbled up, but I clung onto that Bible as though it was a lifeline, a refuge from the spirit I was convinced was trying to kill me.

My mind in turmoil, I paced the floor, wringing my hands, fearful to venture down the stairs. I was frightened in case the 'thing' was still lurking about, ready to pounce on me, or any of my family. I was in mental agony; I knew I couldn't spend the rest of the night in such torture. So I woke Steve up. Holed up in the bathroom, I told him all about what had happened. At first he looked at me a bit sceptically, but he could see that I was fearful, and that something was very wrong with me.

'Listen to me! A ghost got hold of me and was dragging me off the settee.'

He placed his hands on my shoulders. 'OK, son.'

'You have to believe me!'

Nodding, he left the bathroom and headed downstairs. Gingerly, I came behind, scared that what had attacked me might do the same to my stepdad . . . or to both of us.

Standing on the stairs, I watched as he walked into the living room. He switched the light on and looked around. When he came out he said, 'Funny that, it's ice cold in there.' Then he went back into the room and said to the air: 'Get out of here! You are not welcome in this house. Get out, now.'

Shortly after he spoke those words, the temperature returned to normal and the atmosphere became peaceful again. As for me, I couldn't go to sleep. I spent the rest of the night and the early hours of the morning pacing up and down the street. Once the church opened its doors, I went in and spoke to one of the clergy, telling him my dramatic account of the night before. But I felt he didn't believe me; I thought he didn't even understand what I was talking about. John was away for the weekend and I felt very vulnerable. After all, I was in a situation that was hard to share with anyone – it was way beyond the experience of most people.

That evening, I had no intention of going to sleep. Then I had an idea. I called a couple of friends of mine who I knew were committed Christians.

'Please come and see me. I've got a problem and I can't sleep. Can you come and see me?'

I told my friends Hugh and David about the Ouija board, my disturbed sleep and, more importantly, about what had happened to me the previous night.

David said, 'Joe, we are going to pray to God for you in the name of Jesus, that He will give you a good night's sleep, and protect you from evil attacks.'

That night I had the best sleep I'd had for a long time.

Hugh and David came and saw me often over the next few weeks. Their regular praying helped me to sleep, be more in control of myself; it also enabled me to understand the power in Jesus' name and helped me to clearly see that what had happened to me was an attack by evil spirits – unseen but very real.

'Ouija boards, mediums, even horoscopes . . . *anything* that delves into the "unknown" will open doors to evil,' David explained.

I knew what David was telling me was true. I realised that through my dabbling in the Ouija, I had opened these doors . . . and it was affecting my whole life.

7

Set Free

I began to attend church regularly, partly because I felt that I *had* to, but also because singing hymns, listening to sermons and reading my Bible brought me some inner peace.

During the week, I still had great fun with my work colleagues; nothing had changed there. But come the weekend, especially Sunday, I was a 'Christian'.

Every year, many Christians from throughout the UK attend Spring Harvest, a festival that celebrates the Christian faith. This particular year, members of my church were going, so I tagged along with the other young people.

The last night of Spring Harvest was held in the Big Top, a huge tent that held masses of people. It had been a good week for me; I had made some new friends. Also, to see so many Christians together was a bit of a shock – but a nice one.

Gerald Coates, a well-known Christian speaker, was leading the meeting. All the people in the tent were standing, worshipping God. I was tearful, overcome with emotion. An invitation was given for anyone who wanted prayer to come down to the front of the tent. I knew I had to go.

At the front, I knelt down with others, weeping, praying and thanking God. Gerald Coates slowly began to walk towards the people wanting prayer. Suddenly, I was flung onto my back, screaming expletives. A girl from my church came over and tried, unsuccessfully, to pray for me, and a man who was part of the prayer team prayed too – astonishingly, he keeled over and fell on the floor.

Gerald Coates called for someone to pray for me, and a man came over. As he said: 'In the name of Jesus, I command you, unclean spirit, to come out of this man', a loud roar came out of my mouth, followed by uncontrollable belching. I couldn't stop myself. After a time, I started to feel lighter and my head was clearer.

There was real peace in my heart and mind after I went through this episode. The man, who obviously had experience with people like me, explained what had happened.

'Jesus has set you free from the evil spirits that were oppressing you. From now on, you must live for Him if you want to remain free.'

It was an awesome statement. I'd felt I *was* living for Jesus. But I was coming up short somehow!

'What's that video?' I was pointing to a video on my work colleague's desk.

He smiled. 'That's a video of a bunch of ex-debt collectors and East End hard men who've had their lives changed and become Christians.'

Could this be true? I'd thought *my* experiences were weird but, listening to my colleague talking about the video, I was intrigued. I went into the board room and watched it from beginning to end.

When it finished, I sat back, speechless. Then, when at last I found my voice, I said aloud: 'Lord, if there's some way you can get me involved with this group of guys, I really will focus my whole life on you.'

The video showed the guys weightlifting (this was something I was heavily involved in); they were muscular in appearance, they looked liked real men – and they were Christians.

I suddenly remembered a prayer that I had prayed months back, asking God to get me involved in using weights for His glory. And now, here I was, having just watched a video of some guys doing the very same thing!

When I was next at the gym, I was lifting some weights when I noticed a guy whose face I recognised, but I couldn't quite place him. I was training with my friend Chris, who I also worked with. I asked him if he knew the guy.

'Yeah,' said Chris, 'that's Arthur White, World Power-lifting Champion.'

'Do you think you could introduce me to him?'

Chris did just that.

'Hello, Arthur. Can I introduce my mate Joe to you?'

In an East End accent he said, 'Hello, Joe. How are yer, son?' He held out his hand and I shook it. As we began to talk, the penny dropped – this was one of the guys from the video I'd watched!

'Are you the Arthur from the Tough Talk video? You're a Christian?'

He nodded.

'You just aren't going to believe this,' I said, 'but I prayed that I would get involved with you guys.'

'Funnily enough, son, we've been praying for new members.'

I was totally bowled over. God had arranged our meeting!

It wasn't long before I began to attend the Tough Talk prayer meetings. Then I started to go out with the guys – into prisons, schools, town centres, everywhere that Tough Talk was granted a platform to talk about Jesus and encourage people to give their lives to Him. I talked about my experiences with the Ouija board, how I'd thought it was all quite innocent at first. But now I knew it to be far more sinister than I could ever have realised.

Looking back on my life, I know that throughout it all, God has been with me. I was totally unaware of His existence, but Jesus knew me. He knew about all the pain and rejection that I felt at my dad leaving us, when I was young. God was near to me when I was confused about myself and my life, but I didn't know that then. I've wondered why certain things happened (and I still don't have a concrete explanation!) but what I *do* know and believe now is that God cares. He loves me and is watching over all that happens to me.

There is nowhere on this earth that anyone can have a deep, unconditional love except that it comes through faith in Jesus Christ. It may sound crazy, but I have gone through some awful times in my life, things that are beyond human understanding, yet one thing I know for sure – once God has turned His spotlight of love and concern upon a person, that person is never, ever the same again.

And now . . .

'And now, 100 kg British Power-lifting Champion with a new British squat and overall total record – Joe Lampshire.'

The applause was deafening. My jaw was aching from the almost permanent grin on my face. I had done it! I had broken the British championship record. I was overwhelmed. But I knew that without the Lord this would not have been possible for me.

Arthur White had been my spiritual father for a few years. He'd helped me to read and understand the Bible, he'd prayed with me, and was truly a strong, spiritual mentor. He had also coached me; his help in shaping me for power-lifting was invaluable. And he'd introduced me to Alan Simpson, also a British champion in power-lifting. Alan had trained me for the British Championships. He was and still remains an inspiration to me.

The Lord enabled me to not only become the British champion, but I went on to come second in both the European and Commonwealth Championships. All of this, I know, was made possible by having Jesus Christ in my life. Many people say they can do anything without God, but not me. Since I became a Christian, my whole life has been turned round. It's as if I'm a new person, a new Joe, since Jesus came to live in my heart by His powerful Spirit.

The Lord has given me a great amount of physical strength in which I am able to glorify His name as I travel the country, and the world, telling my story. I dread to think what would have happened to me if I hadn't given my life over to Jesus. Would I have ended up deeper into the occult? Would I have tried to escape the horrors in my mind through drugs or alcohol? Would I have sold myself to overwork? But God pulled me out of a terrible situation, giving me hope and forgiveness.

I am married to Denise, and marriage has taken my life to a new level. My wife has helped to stabilise my life, creating a family setting that I could only have dreamed of. Before I was a Christian, women were just objects of desire – love them and leave them. But my attitudes have completely changed; I can see that *all* people are precious and valuable to God. I'm a father, now, too. And as I interact with my son, Joshua, I can also see how God interacts not just with me, but with all who put their trust in Him.

MARTYN PARRISH

1

Wanting Out

'Can you get any Henry?' I asked. I'd seen the guy in front of me many times before at the various squats I frequented.

'Yeah, yeah, I can,' he said. 'It'll take about an hour.'

I shoved my twenty pound note into his hand, careful that no one was watching me. 'I'll be at Kenny's.' I looked the guy straight in the eye as if to say, 'And don't mess me about, otherwise you'll be in big trouble.'

'OK.' He nodded.

I was apprehensive and excited at the same time. Life for a heroin addict, which I was, was growing harder and more dangerous by the minute. Every squat I knew had had more than one visit from the boys in blue. I could be sitting having a chat, after having had a nice fix, when all of a sudden there'd be this loud banging on the front door and we all knew who the callers were. I wasn't one to hang around. I'd locate the back door, and off I went. Jumping garden walls was no problem. Getting arrested was.

At first, sitting in Kenny's was a buzz in itself. The anticipation of getting stoned was worth waiting an hour for. But the hour soon turned into two, and by about three and a half, I knew that I'd been had. The guy had stolen my money and there was no way I could lay my hands on him. Panic kicked in as I thought about what I was going to do to hold off the 'cold turkey' that would soon come if I didn't get some heroin into my body.

I had to go back out on the street again to score. I had to get a fix.

This had become my life. But the police had targeted Hornsey in its drive to oust the dealers and junkies. What was once a sure thing – that you could purchase any type of drug and find a squat to shoot up or whatever it was you did to get drugs into your body – was now very uncertain. Drugs were becoming scarce and dealers were having to make do with their supply. You didn't know what you were getting; you just had to hope for the best, that you weren't getting ripped off.

Even Kenny, who knew every dealer in the vicinity, was finding it difficult to maintain his own habit, let alone supply anyone else.

Many people used Kenny's squat as a place to buy and use. One evening a few of us, Kenny included, were waiting for a batch to come through. I was pacing the room, impatient to get stoned. The atmosphere was tense; we were all in the same boat, frightened, as we could feel sickness slowly coming over us. I walked to the window and froze.

'Come and have a look at this car. Something isn't right.' I pointed to a blue saloon with four men inside. They were looking towards the squat. Instinctively, I knew it was the Old Bill. Rather than take a chance and wait around for my score, I shot out of the first-floor flat, down the stairs and out of the back door.

I'd been right. I found out that the police quickly turned the flat over, whilst some council workers with large hammers smashed the toilet and the sink . . .

Finding another squat was getting harder and harder. But Kenny was like a jack-in-the-box. He always seemed to be able to reinvent himself by getting another squat, spending most of his time finding out who had what, doing deals and getting high. His girlfriend was totally devoted to him. She looked like Debbie Harry, with spiky, uneven blonde hair, red lipstick, leather jacket, and long black lacy gloves disguising her drug use. She would have been a pretty girl but the drugs were beginning to erode her face. Whenever I picked her up from Park Lane where she worked as a prostitute, she would have a stash of money ready to score some gear. It didn't appear to bother her or Kenny that she sold her body to fund their habit. And it didn't bother me that I was like a cabbie, dropping her off and picking her up. Nothing affects junkies, only the getting and taking of drugs to appease the cravings of their mind, body and soul. That was me. Totally single-minded about how I was going to score today.

Truth be told, I was beginning to get tired of the life. I had absolutely no interests apart from heroin. The sun could have dissolved in the sky, or a nuclear bomb could have been dropped, my first priority would have been: 'Where's my next hit coming from?'

I wanted out. But how?

2

Early Years

'Oi, Parrish, this block of wood is just like you!'

Laughter echoed round the woodwork classroom. All eyes were on me, making me feel as though those words were true. Rage coursed through me. A red light burst in my brain and I snatched the chisel off the workbench in front of me, throwing it like a dart towards this boy's head. It missed by a centimetre and hit the wall just above him.

'Parrish, how dare you,' bellowed the teacher. 'Get outside, right now.'

As I walked towards the classroom door, the anger began to disappear. Standing in the corridor, head bent as the teacher berated me for my bad behaviour, I felt terrible. Normally, I was quite an easy-going person. But during this last year at school, everything seemed to fuel the frustration and resentment I felt because of my inability to read and write properly. Most of my teachers complained about why I couldn't do the 'simple' work, but no one ever tried to find out (or explain to me) why my reading and writing skills were so poor – something which affected all my young life.

Now I was being frogmarched to the headmaster's office for a good telling off, or worse.

'So, Parrish, you think you can use our tools as deadly missiles, do you? Hold out your hand, boy.'

Whack! The wooden ruler struck my palms several times. I wanted to rub my hands against my trouser leg to stop them stinging so much, but I fronted it out and tried to be brave.

'Parrish,' the headmaster went on, 'this type of behaviour is totally unacceptable in my school. I have a good mind to stop you competing in all sports as from today.'

My heart froze. 'Stop all sports? You can't do that! That's my life, that'll be the end of me!' I wanted to shout those words out, but I couldn't. I just stood there, feeling shocked. The headmaster's lips were moving but I couldn't take in what he was saying. I lived for sports. I loved the tackle, the rough and tumble of rugby; I was one of the smallest in the class, but what I lacked in height I made up for in tenacity and determination. Athletics enabled me to work off huge amounts of energy as I tore around the track; long jump liberated my mind as I propelled myself into the bed of sand. I was a bit of hero when it came to sporting events, competing on behalf of the school, winning medals and cups. But now, the unthinkable was about to happen! Or was it?

'. . . to hear any bad reports about you again this term. Do you understand, Parrish? Or I will bar you from all sporting events – no matter how good you are.' The headmaster's piercing eyes met mine and I wanted to squirm. Clenching my fists, which were still painful, I stood still, holding my breath and not moving a muscle.

'You can go now, but remember, I am watching you.'

'Here, have one of mine.'

I shook my packet of Rothmans and my mate took a cigarette and stuck it in his mouth.

'Ta, mate.' He inhaled deeply and blew a lungful of smoke out. He coughed and inhaled again.

I took the last drag from my cigarette and ground it out with the toe of my boot.

'Mart, give us that panel hammer, mate.'

I rummaged through the huge toolbox on the floor and handed it to him.

I had been working at a garage doing car repairs for a few months since leaving school. It was like entering another world. There was hardly any reading and writing involved in the job, and I was glad about that.

It was funny really, but I had gone from sports training every night, to nothing. At school what I lacked in the classroom, I made up for on the track. Once school was over, that was it . . . It was a bit frightening, really. One minute I was a boy in school, being told what I could and could not do and, within a short space of time, I was a man, working and earning money. And smoking!

I'd had no vices when I was at school – I suppose because I wanted to be fit and healthy so I had a good chance of winning. But now, that was all behind me. I had entered the real world.

Smoking came easy. All the guys I worked with smoked. It made perfect sense to me to smoke as well. I was usually the outsider in school, but here, with real men, I was just one of them.

'Fancy a pint after work, Mart?' asked one of the guys.

I nodded. 'Yeah, that'll be great.' I wasn't really much of a drinker but again, I liked the fact that I was being included and accepted for who I was. So it was easy to say yes.

The pub wasn't far from the garage, and there were usually quite a few workmen there, having a couple of pints before going home. It was a great smoky, boozy atmosphere.

I was lucky to have landed the job at the garage. My brother Graham was a mechanic and he knew someone who knew someone else that needed an apprentice. Standing in the pub, I remembered a teacher who told me, 'You won't amount to anything, Parrish. You won't even be able to get a job at the rate you're going,' and I wanted to laugh. I had a job and a good one at that!

'Here, mate, pick a horse and I'll treat you to a bet.'

We were at the bar as my mate shoved a newspaper into my hand. It felt as if my heart rate doubled as I scanned the page. I couldn't read a thing. The words seemed all jumbled up and back to front, nothing made sense. Panic welled up in me. I didn't know what to do. Somehow, my voice squeaked out, 'Nah, save yer money. There's nothing there I fancy.' And so I was able to bluff my way out.

As I left the pub, I breathed a sigh of relief – yet again I had escaped. I'd had many 'near misses' like that, where I was put on the spot to read something and couldn't do it. In truth, I felt like a freak. Everyone I knew could read and write, except me. I wasn't going to waste my life trying to work out why, but sometimes, just sometimes, I'd feel my guts pulling every which way as I struggled in situations I wasn't equipped to handle. Once, Graham handed me a motoring magazine. He was a rally driver and was forever competing, so naturally he'd want his younger brother to know what he'd been up to.

'Here, Mart, have a look at this. What do you think? I'm on page 24. Do you think it's true what they said?'

My hands trembled as I took the magazine. I stared at the page but, as always, the words intermingled and merged together. What was *wrong* with me? Everyone could read, couldn't they? Why couldn't I?

I held onto the magazine long enough to make my brother think that I had read the article, and then I handed it back to him.

'Why didn't you read it out?' he asked.

'And make your head swell twice the size it is already?'

Graham laughed. I chuckled but it was false laughter. Really, I wanted to cry, but I held my emotions in check. I was determined that no one would ever know about my problem – not even my brother! It was my secret.

'That's a beauty, ain't it?' I looked lovingly at the beautiful, sleek, red and chrome body of my new bike. It was a Triumph 250cc and cost me a month's wages. Riding it away from the showroom filled me with confidence and power. Roaring through the streets I felt invincible, more than flesh and blood.

Working at the garage was an all-man's world. It was on a complex with other garages. Dean, who was about the same age as me, worked a few doors away. He was taller than me, with shoulder-length brown hair, and laughing brown eyes. We soon got together and met up during the weekend.

'Cor, your bike shines up a real treat, Mart!' he said.

I was pleased with his compliment. I felt like a proud parent with a talented child. We stood looking at our bikes for a short while. Dean's older brother, Craig, pulled into the kerb behind our bikes. Jumping out of his car, he came and stood next to us; he had long hair parted down the middle, and it never looked as if he brushed it.

'They look right good, those bikes,' he said, looking at our machines. Then he nodded his head towards the house. 'Fancy a toke, boys?' He placed his two fingers in front of his mouth and blew out imaginary smoke.

Rubbing his hands together, Dean said, 'Count me in.'

I wasn't quite sure if I wanted 'in', but shrugged and followed them into their house. Both their parents were away for the day, so we had the place to ourselves. Craig cleared the kitchen table of clutter and, with a placemat in front of him, emptied his pockets, putting the stuff on the mat – a packet of Rizlas, a packet of Rothmans, and a block covered in foil. Dean and I watched as Craig expertly rolled the 'skins' (the cigarette papers) together without any of the substances falling out. Craig flicked his lighter and inhaled as the end crackled and fired up. He handed it to Dean. Then it was my turn.

I inhaled as though I was smoking an ordinary cigarette, and passed it back to Craig.

'Lebanese. Black gold, it's called. Worth it's weight, too,' laughed Craig.

I agreed with him. Craig made a few more 'spliffs' (cannabis cigarettes, also called 'joints') and, by the time we had smoked them, I was feeling *so* chilled. It was as though some peace bomb from outer space had been dropped into my brain. I felt cool and together and like I wasn't bothered about a thing. I decided I must try this again, and it wasn't long before I was buying my own 'draw' (cannabis) and rolling my own spliffs.

My parents, brother and sister didn't smoke or drink. My family were light years away from anything like that. My parents' main concern was that I was in work. Work was important to them; they both worked *very* hard, running a newsagent's. Early in the morning, Dad was up sorting out the papers and magazines, and he didn't stop until the shop shut later that evening. I loved my parents, but they didn't have time to watch my every move; I was a bit of a free spirit and I could more or less do as I pleased. My brother Graham was five years older than me and my sister Janice, four. To be honest, we didn't have a lot in common. It wasn't as though we were strangers to each other, but we had different interests. And mine was to lead me in a dark and dangerous direction.

3

Living for the Weekends

I stood outside the back door of my house, lazily watching the sun set. My parents had gone out to dinner and I had the whole house to myself. Great!

Sitting in a garden chair, I expertly rolled up a joint. Glancing around, I checked that none of the neighbours were in their gardens. I didn't want to have the Old Bill banging on my door and carting me off to the police station because some nosy neighbour had seen me smoking illegal drugs.

Lighting the end of the joint and taking the first toke (smoke) was, as ever, pure bliss. Usually, after a joint, I would ride my bike to the local pub and have a couple of half pints of cider. Cannabis did not adversely affect my life – or so I thought. It just made me feel calm, chilled, soothed. Apart from that, everything was just the same. Working was no problem for me. Riding my bike up and down the road was a breeze. I was cautious about drinking more than I should, because I knew that alcohol did affect you, especially when driving or riding vehicles, so I was careful about that; yet, strangely, I did not think smoking drugs altered your mind (and neither did my friends). I know now that what it *does* do is give you a false sense of well-being that can lure you down a very narrow, self-harming and suicidal road.

Soon, smoking joints became a way of life. To me, it was the same as smoking cigarettes – it just cost a bit more.

'You going out again, Martyn? Dad and I never see you these days,' said Mum.

'I'm a young man, Mum. I've got to do what I've got to do,' I laughed.

Mum smiled and left me to get myself ready to go out. I wasn't particularly fashion conscious – jeans, motor-cycle boots, leather jacket and white shirt, finished off with a splash of Brut. I had been growing my hair since I left school, and it was now down my back. I thought I looked cool!

Every weekend I was usually out and about with Dean. One Friday night, while we were drinking and having a good time at a pub in Chingford, I saw Craig drop some blue pills into Dean's hand. Dean swallowed them down with a swig of cider.

Craig caught me looking and said, "'Ere, you want some?'

I was hesitant. Smoking joints was one thing, but tak-ing pills was completely out of my range. What kind of effect would they have on me? I knew people died from taking pills. Would I be sick all over the place? Would I end up crazy and paranoid?

Then an inexplicable feeling seemed to overwhelm me.

'OK,' I said. 'I'll have a few.'

It took Craig a few seconds to pop the lid of a camera film pot and shake out six little blue tablets into the palm of my hand. My heart was thudding; I didn't really want to take them, but the feeling of being left out of my loop of friends was a strong incentive. I swallowed the pills with some cider. Nothing happened for a while and I began to relax. Then the band came on – long-haired rockers who were screaming down the mikes, twanging on their guitars, busting up the drums – and I could feel my pulse begin to vibrate faster and faster. I went to the middle of the dance floor, something that I had never done before, and began to jump higher than anyone else, twisting and shaking as though I had been plugged into the electric mains. Sweat was bursting out of every pore; soon I was drenched in perspiration. My hair was stuck to my face and I knew I looked a mess but I didn't care. When the music stopped my heart rate was still working overtime.

'Hey, Dean, do you want a drink?' I asked, as I lit a cigarette. He was wiping sweat from his eyes with the arm of his leather jacket.

'Yeah, I'll have a pint this time.'

At the bar I got chatting to a couple of girls. They were laughing, putting their hands over their mouths, as I gabbled on and on. I couldn't stop myself. Never in my life had I been able to hold a solid conversation with a girl, much less *girls*. A bit unsteadily, I took the drinks back to where Dean was standing. He and I started talking a load of rubbish – totally banal, senseless *rubbish*. But our mouths couldn't stay shut and our bodies couldn't be still. Then the pub called last orders, and I was surprised. The time had gone by very quickly. I felt as though I had been in the pub for just a couple of minutes.

'Mart, what shall we do?'

I looked at Dean and burst out laughing. I was clutching my sides, doubling over with inane laughter. It wasn't long before Dean joined in. We staggered out of the pub, holding on to each other, laughing for no reason. The more I tried to get a grip on myself, the more my mind seemed scrambled. Climbing on my bike, I turned the ignition, kick-started the machine and it roared into life.

As the bike picked up speed, my face was cooled by the night air, and my mind began to clear as I sort of sobered up. Leaning forward as the bike swerved and thundered along country lanes, it was as though I was moulded to the seat. I felt a surge of power; it seemed as if I had become larger than life itself. It was heady stuff and, of course, I wanted to do it again. I wanted to drop (take) some pills and then ride my bike. This was living! Or so I thought. And so I fell into a pattern of going to work normally during the week, but at the weekends smoking cannabis and dropping blues on Friday and Saturday nights. I felt as if I was a free spirit, enjoying this stage of my uncluttered life, free from responsibility. I had not one iota of hassle from my parents. As far as they were concerned, I was working hard and keeping out of trouble. When I was under the influence of drugs (even though I didn't feel as though I was influenced in any way), I appeared to be totally in command of my life. I wasn't falling down, being sick or acting in a violent way. I was 'a cool guy'. Life at the weekends was party-time, and I lived it to the full.

A few months later, I was introduced to another drug.

Our supplier was a guy named Philip, who lived alone. He had dark circles under his eyes; he looked as though he didn't get much sleep, and his frame was skeletal. He was a lot older than Dean and me, and he was able to supply whatever we needed.

It was a cold Friday evening in February. The dampness never affected me because, I suppose, thoughts of smoking, pill-popping and drinking seemed to keep me warm. After running up two flights of stairs, we banged on Philip's door. He let us in, and sat down at his table.

Then he rolled up a ten pound note, held it over some white powder that was in a line, snorted it, and wiped his nose on the back of his hand.

Dean held out a tenner and said, 'We'll have some blues, mate.'

Taking a mouthful from his bottle of lager, Philip replied, 'Sorry, I'm out, fellas. But you can have some of this.' He pointed to a plastic bag with small paper parcels inside.

'What is it?' I asked.

'Sulphate. Brilliant stuff. I know you'll like it.'

I began to feel a bit edgy. I had quickly got used to rolling cannabis and swallowing the blue pills, but this white powder stuff was way over the top. I remembered seeing television pictures of people out of their skulls; celebrities had *died* through this sort of drug abuse. Snorting white powder up your nose to get a high? No way! I was shaking my head, but I heard Dean's voice.

'It's only a couple quid more, I'll stand that.'

I really, *really* didn't want to touch the stuff. One of the main reasons was that I didn't want to snort anything up my nose. Noses were for breathing! What if something went wrong and I couldn't breathe? I'd be dead! Then again, I didn't want to be thought a wimp and find myself outside of my group of friends. So I nodded.

Dean, who had taken this stuff before, snorted a line. Then Philip – who must have seen me shaking my head before – said to me, 'Don't worry about it. Look.' And he showed me how to take it a different way. I did as he said, but nothing happened.

After paying Philip, we left for the pub. All the way there I was waiting for something to happen – zilch. An hour later, I was complaining to Dean, 'This stuff is weak. I can't feel a thing.' The music was beating out and usually by now I would be in the middle of the floor doing my thing. Instead I was on the outskirts, watching the fun pass me by.

'C'mon,' said Dean. 'Let's go to the loos.'

Squeezing into a loo, Dean cleaned the top of the cistern with the palm of his hand. I was less nervous of snorting it now because I thought what I had already taken was near useless. Dean had the first hit and I followed suit. Nothing again.

'Waste of money, this, mate,' I said. 'Give me blues any day.'

Dean grinned.

Within minutes of entering the dance area I felt as though my head was going to blow right off my neck. I jumped into the middle of the dance floor; the whole of my body was jumping, I felt as if I was on another level. When the music stopped, I stopped dancing, but it felt as if I was covered in little hammers that were tap, tap, tapping away at me. My heart was racing, I couldn't stand completely still. My mouth was very dry. I pushed my way towards the bar, gulped down a cider and ordered another.

The music came on again, and I grabbed my drink, making my way over to Dean. We began laughing and acting stupid. Dancing, I was shaking my body, flailing my arms, getting lost in my mind and the music. When the music stopped again, I kept going. Dean came and tapped me on the shoulder – it was a few moments before I responded.

'You all right, Mart?'

Running my hands across my sweaty face I nodded. 'This sulphate stuff is good, real good.'

I walked towards the bar for another cider and saw other people who had been popping pills and worse. Even though it was dark, with flashing lights, I knew that most people were high on something, and it wasn't fresh air – they were chatting and laughing non-stop, acting just like me. Sipping my drink, I felt at one with every single person in the pub. The outside world was far away. This was real life. This was where it was all happening.

Weekends began to get more and more intense and I was finding it difficult to swing back to normal life on Monday mornings. Sheer determination got me crawling out of bed. The downside of my drug-taking weekends was absolute physical exhaustion. My whole body wanted to shut down so it could recuperate and get me ready to face the world. But that might take a couple of days, and work was calling, so I had to go. There were times when I was late, the boss would have a go, and it wouldn't have taken much for me to turn around and walk out. But my parents had drilled into me the importance of working for a living. So I'd mumble an apology and begin work. I'd have a thick head the whole day and, when I got home, I'd sneak down to the end of the garden and have a joint so that I could start to feel 'myself' again, all the while nervously looking around in case either my parents or my neighbours caught me.

I was getting paranoid. Yet, I lived for my weekends and the drugs I was taking. I wasn't going to give *them* up, or my friends, so I would have to find a way to overcome the bad Monday mornings.

4

The Slippery Slope

My life had settled into a pattern of work, riding my bike, pubbing, smoking weed and taking sulphate. I had no inclination or desire to alter anything in my life. And then I met Eddie.

Eddie was a tall, thin guy. He had few tattoos on each arm and an earring in his left ear – most bikers wore the same sort of 'uniform'. The difference with Eddie was that he really knew about narcotics; he was a connoisseur. And, more importantly, he was able to procure all sorts of drugs that I had never thought about trying.

Friday was a hot night in the pub. Dean and me and a few others had been snorting sulphate and were in a very happy mood. Then Eddie came over.

"Ere,' said Eddie. 'Last week I went on a fantastic trip.'

'Where did you go, abroad?' I said.

He burst out laughing and we all joined in. I didn't know what we were laughing at but he was laughing really hard and we were all high, so it just seemed natural.

'No, you nut,' he said, with a big grin on his face. 'I mean I had some LSD and it was the business.'

I was intrigued. The fear of trying new drugs was gone; I was up for anything. Dean said, 'Can you get us some, mate?'

'Yeah, no problem.'

We arranged to meet up at High Beach, part of Epping Forest, not far from my home. Quite convenient!

I spent Saturday morning cleaning my bike and in the evening, Dean and I met up with some friends, chatting, smoking, drinking beer from cans. It was a good, cheapish evening. I had a real sense of belonging to this crowd. We were roughly the same age, interested in our bikes, drinking and smoking. It was like being a member of a family with lots of brothers and a few sisters.

That Sunday morning was bright. I remember feeling really good as the sun's rays streamed through my curtains. My parents were working and my brother and sister were no longer living at home. So I was alone.

I liked my own company a lot, but there were times when I wanted to be closer to someone, to have some kind of affinity with them. I was sure that's what families should be like. It wasn't that my family weren't close; it just felt as though we were a bit like ships passing in the night . . . or day. My parents were busy running the shop, and I only really saw them if I was home during the early evening, or at Sunday lunch.

Craig and Dean picked me up in their car in the early afternoon, and we made our way to High Beach. It was quite hot and I basked on the back seat getting high on the weather – with a little cannabis.

The car park was packed, so it took some time to find a space. I was sweating as I clambered out the car, and relieved to breathe the cool, fresh air. We quickly found a group of our mates who were already into the swing of things. They were sitting on the grass in a sort of circle, cans of beer stacked in the middle. A radio was blaring out heavy rock music. Saying our hellos, Dean added our cans to the pile. I plonked myself down, and began to secretly roll a joint. High Beach is heavily populated with families during nice weather, and although I could see most of the adults were taken up with their off-spring, I felt I had to be careful. I didn't want an irate parent seeing me 'skinning up' or the next thing I knew I'd be surrounded by police!

Lighting the joint, I took a deep toke. It was good stuff and after a few more puffs I could feel the familiar calm-ness wash over me. I passed it to Dean. It seemed a pleasant way to pass a Sunday afternoon.

Eddie effortlessly slipped into our circle and began drinking some beer. He was with a few other guys, and everyone seemed glad to see him, including me. We all knew that he would have some stuff on him and I want-ed to try out LSD. He had described the effect that the drug had on him and I thought it would be a laugh to experience it for myself.

Crouching down, Eddie pulled a small plastic bag from his pocket. He began to hand out the contents as people handed over their money. I was a bit disappoin-ted when I first saw the LSD pill. It was brown, and the same size as a match head.

'We've been had,' I murmured to Dean. 'That ain't much of a tablet, what's that gonna do?'

Dean smiled. 'Don't be fooled by the size of it. It's what it contains . . . *that's* what should concern you.'

At first, nothing happened. But now I was a bit more clued up, I knew that sometimes it did take a while for a drug to begin to flow in your bloodstream and you felt the effects.

Within an hour the tablet was hitting its mark. Dusk began to settle and my head felt very heavy. I knew I was stoned, really stoned. It was a nice feeling to be free of thoughts and worries. You see, that's what drugs do at first; free up your mind . . . before taking over completely.

'Hey guys, we're wasting this trip just sitting here. Let's take a walk, right?' shouted Eddie.

Slowly, people began to stand up. It was difficult for me. I could hardly hold my head up, let alone stand up. Dean had to help me. Once on my feet, I started to put one foot in front of the other. It felt as though something had happened to my legs. Or maybe it wasn't my legs, it was the ground. It had gone all spongy, like a large mattress, and it made walking difficult.

'What's going on?' I was frightened that I was going to fall, but I could feel Dean holding on to me.

As we walked towards the trees, it was as though I was seeing them for the first time. Something was telling my brain, 'Of *course* I've seen trees – many times!' But not under the influence of LSD; I felt like the artist Picasso – seeing ordinary, everyday objects in a different way. As we got closer to the forest, the colours became more intense and vivid, as though the colour button on the TV had been turned up. Squinting, I tried to focus to get the picture in front of me back into line. But the trees began to change into Disney cartoon shapes. The long branches grew arms and hands and waved them at me, bending low. It scared the life out of me.

'No, no!'

I felt Dean tug on my arm. 'It's all right, mate, keep it together.'

It was fine for him to tell me that, but as far as I could see, the trees had come alive. The evening was getting darker, and it seemed as though the darkness was moulding around the trees. My surroundings were getting smaller and smaller, closing in on me. My heart was beating quicker now and my lungs were pushing air out twice as fast as usual. I felt a sense of panic, but Dean's firm hand on my arm enabled me to suppress the feeling somehow.

Deeper into the forest, my perception of what was happening around me intensified. I was stepping on twigs and pebbles and the sound was overwhelming as each footfall crunched and snapped the forest debris. The gentle wind that blew through the leaves sounded as though it had taken on a persona of its own; it was like a tangible being. It seemed to howl and whistle; the whole atmosphere became spooky and I wanted to turn and run, but I couldn't. My legs were doing their own thing and it took all my energy to keep up with the group. Somewhere in the forest we managed to find a log and sit down. I felt a little better, safer, as we huddled together as a group. But as soon as we started walking, the weird sensations began again. It was hours before we came out of the forest and were in the open. Walking up the steep hill towards the car park, a sobering feeling began to steady me. At the top, we were able to see Chingford in its night-time glory. The street and domestic lights gave the town a kind of unreal glow. It looked like Toy Town; the houses had shrunk to minuscule sizes.

We walked to the car, laughing and joking. There were a few couples in parked cars, but they weren't interested in us and we weren't interested in them. We stood around, smoking cigarettes and drinking the last of the beer, sharing our latest drug-induced experiences. My mind was groggy on the drive home. The 'trip' had ended but I was not yet myself. I was very, very tired and it seemed as though all the power of thought had been wiped from my mind. It was such an effort to think so I just didn't. By the time I walked up to my front door and inserted the key, I was completely whacked.

Climbing into bed seemed a monumental effort because I had to *think* about lifting up my legs and swinging them under the blankets.

My sleep was punctuated by mini flashbacks of my hallucinations. I was restless, tossing and turning the whole night. Just when I thought I would get a decent couple of hours, a bright light would flash into my mind and then a series of colours and shapes would buzz around. It was crazy. Consequently, by the morning I was exhausted. The alarm kicked off and it sounded like Big Ben exploding in my head. It was hard for me to even think about going to work, but I knew I'd have to get my act together somehow.

I had been working in the garage for about three years. I was happy to have passed my driving test and was now the proud owner of a car. That morning, it seemed easier for me to use my car rather than my bike. I'd had a few narrow escapes whilst riding my bike – nothing major, just a couple of broken fingers and grazed legs, 'road rash' – when I was under the influence. So I reckoned the car would be a much safer option. Besides, I kept my bike in pristine condition, and it upset me if it got a little scratch. I wasn't about to risk it today. But I couldn't start the car. I turned the key in the ignition again and again, but it was dead. Then I realised the battery was flat. I should have got it sorted over the weekend, but of course I was as high as a kite, and getting a new battery was far from my mind.

Flagging down another motorist, I got him to help me jump-start the car. It coughed into life and away I went. Noise was still a bit accentuated for me, so passing traffic sounded as though it was inside my head. The tiredness gripping my body was getting worse, not better. To top it all, I was going to be late for work again because I would have to stop for petrol.

I nosed my car onto the forecourt of the petrol station, jumped out, grabbed the nozzle, and jammed it into my tank.

'Hey, mate, turn the engine off.'

Ignoring the voice, I continued to fill up.

'Did you hear me? Turn it off! Do you want us to blow up or something?'

A young man wearing overalls came towards me, pointing and shouting. I had seen him before and knew that he was the guy who put petrol in your car as you waited patiently. Today, I hadn't got the time. That's why I was doing it myself. He came right up to me and tried to wrestle the petrol nozzle out of my hand. I whacked him. He fell down with a thud.

I had nearly finished putting enough petrol into my tank to get me to work and back home, when the guy jumped up. I was exasperated. If only he'd give me a minute, I'd soon be done! But no, he tried to stop me once more. So I gave him a good left and right hook that knocked him to the ground again. This time he couldn't get up.

Placing the nozzle back on the stand, I went into the kiosk to pay. The minutes were ticking past, and I was more than late for work now. A man took my money, giving me a wary look. It didn't bother me. I threw my money down on the counter and left. The petrol pump attendant was still on the ground, groaning. I walked past him. As far as I was concerned, it was *his* fault for behaving in the way that he did. It hadn't taken me long to fill up. He should have left me alone.

Slamming the door, I headed off the forecourt. Then a police car appeared. It stopped, blocking the exit.

The man from the kiosk was out on the forecourt, shouting, 'It's him! He's the one. He's needs locking up!' And I watched as a policeman got out of the car and ran towards me.

I was handcuffed and taken to Waltham Abbey Police Station, spending nearly the whole day in a pokey cell. My dad's shop was only across the road, yet he didn't know what had happened. And there I was, whiling away my time, losing money for missing a day's work. When my dad eventually found out where I was, he came to pick me up.

'What stupid thing do you think you were doing?' he demanded. 'Why didn't you just turn your engine off? What was the problem? You've got to learn to control your temper!'

Shrugging, I couldn't say anything. 'It's a bit too late now,' I thought to myself. Yeah, I knew I was in the wrong. But I'd been in a hurry, hadn't I?

Fighting was something I did from time to time, to sort a matter out. Mostly, I was able to keep my temper in check, but when I didn't, I usually lashed out and, whatever the problem was, it was settled *my* way.

Today, my altered state of mind, coupled with my temper, had made sure I was going to end up with a police record. I was charged with Actual Bodily Harm, bound over to keep the peace for a year, and had to pay £250. Yes, I was well and truly on the slippery slope.

5

Smack

By now, I was quite acclimatised to my drug-taking life. I had no direction, no ambitions to achieve anything. I was happy to just coast along, taking each day as it came. All the people I hung out with were much the same as me. We enjoyed each other's company, did the same things. There was still no great interaction between my parents and me, and I kept myself out of trouble, especially since the petrol station incident.

Since leaving school, I'd just worked on cars, and I was getting a bit fed up. I don't know why I did it, but I applied for a position at a plant nursery, delivering soil.

I got the job, and after a short test, was out delivering. It was great to be out on the road instead of cooped up in a greasy garage. I was driving 3500-weight vehicles, worked alone, and it was great. Most of the delivery jobs were reasonably local – Hertfordshire: Broxbourne, Stevenage – not too far from home. It was nice to drive along the country lanes in control of a large vehicle. I felt free from the restraints of life. Sometimes, I would have a sneaky puff which would bring an added sense of peace and tranquillity. I loved the life so much I thought that if I got my HGV licence, I could travel further afield

. . . maybe even on the Continent. I began to seriously consider taking the necessary steps to get my licence.

A few months later, I was speeding through the nursery. I had one hand on the steering wheel and my other arm was casually resting on the window. In hindsight, if I had been paying attention whilst driving, my life might have taken a different course. But, unfortunately, the lorry wheel clipped a pipe which caused the steering wheel to be yanked out of my hand. And because of my speed, I lost control of the lorry and crashed into one of the large industrial greenhouses. Burst pipes began to spray water all over the place. Shocked, I quickly climbed down from the cab, and joined in with the rest of the staff, trying to salvage at least some of the African violets. Consequently, I could no longer be trusted to drive the lorries and was given mundane jobs to do on the nursery premises. This soon got on my nerves and I left, taking my dreams of driving abroad with me.

It wasn't long before I got another job, working with cars again. My job was to prepare vehicles for sale. If a car had a scratch or a small dent, I would sort it out. The boss would take me to car auctions and, between us, we would look over cars. If we bought one, I'd drive it back to the garage, knowing what needed to be done to it.

I had sold my bike as it was becoming too dangerous for me to ride it. I was having more accidents because of my drug-taking, and I reasoned that it might not be long before I was really unlucky and lost my life. As soon as I got the money in my hand from the sale of the bike, I blew it on a 'drug feast' and was totally out of my head for ages. But one of the perks of my new job was that I could drive different cars home. So, unlike my mates, who were driving old bangers, I was able to drive high-performance sports models or luxury executive cars.

I loved driving. Because I didn't like drinking alcohol much, I would ferry my friends about from pubs to parties and back home, where we would smoke a 'bong'.

Eddie became more and more a part of my group of friends, and I would meet up with him at the pub or at the garage that Graham owned – by now, he had his own business. Eddie was a ladies' man; girls would flock to him and he loved it. And, of course, it was good to have him around because he was also our supplier.

One evening, straight from work, I made my way to the garage to meet Eddie. I had smoked my last joint that afternoon and I needed a draw. Recently, there had been a cannabis shortage and it was getting harder to score.

'Hey, Eddie, got any draw?' I had just pulled into the garage in my borrowed, almost new, Lotus Cortina.

'Ain't got nothing, mate. Everywhere round here is dry.' Eddie eyed the car. 'I know where I can get my hands on some, though.' He smiled. 'But I need some wheels.'

'Hop in, I'll take you there.'

I collected money from others who wanted a draw, and off we went. It was the first of many visits to Hornsey, north London. Eddie introduced me to an Irish couple who looked like hippies left over from the Sixties. They lived in a squat above a launderette. The windows were grimy, with old sheets for curtains, and the main room had a bed in the corner, a couple of armchairs with no stuffing, and a few cushions scattered on the floor. The carpet was an indescribable colour. It was filthy, but when you are hooked on drugs, you don't care.

The Irish couple's accents were so strong I couldn't understand them at first, but we soon began to talk a universal language when the big bag of cannabis was put on the table.

'. . . tea?' asked the woman, whose name was Colleen. I didn't fully understand what she had said, but when I heard the word 'tea' I nodded and smiled.

Soon, we were puffing on some very good resin. There were constant knocks on the door, and customers would seek to purchase whatever drugs they wanted. Some would stay and chat, smoke or inhale. Others, desperate for a hit, would buy and quickly leave so that they could take their drugs and reach a high alone.

Stowing the ounce of cannabis down the front of my trousers, I was smiling to myself as we came out of Fergus and Colleen's. I had paid £35 for the ounce, and three of my mates had given me £10 each, which meant that they would get a quarter of an ounce each. I had only paid a fiver myself and still had my quarter ounce sorted for the week. This was the beginning of a lucrative business for me. I would often go with Eddie to Hornsey to buy drugs for myself and friends, and I was able to either get my drugs for free or for less money. It was a good way for me to support my drug habit on the cheap. I started to make a name for myself; people in my area who wanted cannabis knew they could come to me and I would score for them. I was happy to do this; it was a nice feeling, being wanted. It boosted my social life and increased my drug intake. And through Eddie, I made a lot of friends who sold drugs, too.

It wasn't long before I was going to Hornsey alone. I knew where most of the drug dealers lived and what I couldn't get from one dealer, I would usually pick up from another. Driving different cars was an added bonus, because if the police ever got wind of my shady transactions, they wouldn't be able to tail me.

I would take any drug that was offered to me. I mainly used cannabis and a bit of speed or sulphate. LSD was not really my drug of choice, although sometimes I would

have a trip. But the flashbacks and the fact that it took so
long to get stoned – and for the effects to wear off – meant
I took it the least.

I was getting an order from Fergus and Colleen's with
one of my casual girlfriends, Susanna. When Fergus
opened the door, he looked very stoned, and said in his
strong accent, 'I got some great tablets here now, try one.'

'How much are they and what are they?'

'They're a pound each and they're morph pills.'

I bought one for myself and one for Susanna. I swallowed my pill with a mouthful of tea, the hot liquid
dissolving the tablet quickly. I was sitting on the floor,
talking and laughing, and then I felt myself drifting off
into a daydream. I fell asleep and didn't wake up until
the next morning. The morphine tablet was so powerful
that it had induced sleep almost instantly. It had the
opposite effect on my girlfriend; she was buzzing.

For the next couple of weekends, I was taking morphine and smoking cannabis. And, within a matter of
weeks, another new drug entered my life. Heroin. At
that time, it was commonly called 'smack' (also known
as Henry, H, and other names). Most people I'd met
through purchasing drugs at the different squats in
Hornsey were taking it in various forms, and it seemed
natural for me to do likewise.

I first experienced heroin one Friday evening, when
Susanna and I decided to spend some time with Fergus
and Colleen at their squat. It was strange, really;
Susanna's parents were wealthy, living in a large house
with a swimming pool, and my own parents were not
short of a bob or two; yet here we both were, leaving our
respectable homes to live the filthy, seedy, illegal drug-
taking life.

Knocking on Fergus's door, we had to wait a while for
him to answer it. I could hear him groaning. When at

last he opened the door, I could see he was completely out of his head. How he managed to recognise us I don't know, but we followed him into the flat and found Colleen on the settee, barely able to open her eyes. She managed to mumble something I took to be a greeting.

'What's happening, Ferg?' I asked.

He sat on the floor and ran his fingers through his hair. 'Chasing the dragon, that's what's happening,' he said.

They were both absolutely stoned. Everything they did was in slow motion. I wanted some of that. As Susanna made some tea, I patiently listened to Fergus. He told me how he and Colleen had been indulging in smack. I persuaded him to take me to another dealer who had some heroin to sell, because Fergus and Colleen had smoked their stack.

Fergus took me to a street a short walk away from where he lived. It was lined with derelict houses, about to be demolished. He told me we were going to see a South African guy, a drug dealer who lived on the second floor of what had once been a large, imposing house. Fergus threw pebbles up at the window, the curtain twitched and, a few seconds later, the front door opened.

Kenny was very skinny, with pale skin and ginger hair. It took me a while to understand his accent, but Fergus had no trouble conversing with him, and soon we were heading back towards Fergus's flat.

After another cup of tea, we all sat on the floor as Fergus opened up the 'wrap' of smack. Susanna went first. The hit was instant. She leaned back against the settee, closing her eyes with a smile on her face. I was eager to go next. Immediately, an overwhelming feeling, just like a tidal wave, engulfed me, and I felt very relaxed, like I was floating on air. But after the initial high, my mind and body were craving to do it again. But I was unable to move. I was stoned.

A few hours later I was driving home.

'We have to do that again, Martyn. That was an incredible high,' said Susanna, as I dropped her outside her house.

'Yeah.' Even though the effects of the smack had worn off, I was still a bit in twilight land. The rapid high that I'd had was mind-blowing. Never in all of my drug-taking experience had I had a reaction like that. I thought about how many people had said smack was addictive; but then, people had told me that other drugs were addictive, too, and they weren't – well, not for me. Or so I thought. To be honest, heroin was something I thought I could either take or leave. I was not injecting the drug into my body; I was 'harmlessly' smoking it, so it wasn't much different to smoking cannabis, was it . . . although the effects were quicker and lasted longer . . . For me, it just wasn't frightening to think that I was taking a highly addictive drug.

The desire for the drug was insidious. I was planning to go back to Hornsey the following weekend but it was the following *day* that Susanna and I were heading back to north London.

'Sorry, mate, I'm out. Let's go to Kenny's,' drawled Fergus.

We walked quickly until we got to Kenny's place. Then, back at the squat, we replayed the scene from the day before, with Susanna going first. It was the same again for me . . . or nearly. The hit was high but not as high as yesterday. I was not able to totally control my body, and I had a slightly stronger craving for more smack so I could achieve that first high.

Monday morning, I was back at work as though nothing unusual had happened to me over the weekend. But the truth was I felt really under the weather; it had taken all of my strength to get out of bed and ready for work. My body was aching and I felt as though I was getting the flu. I struggled through the day, trying to get my work done. I had to force myself to bring the car I was working on up to scratch. That whole week seemed to stretch on forever. It did become easier to cope, but I was really looking forward to the weekend so that I could indulge myself in some more smack. And that's what I did. For the next month or so, Susanna and I spent our weekends with Fergus and Colleen, smoking heroin.

One weekend, we scored at a local pub close to where Fergus and Colleen lived. It was a known haunt for drug dealers and junkies. At the flat, Susanna went first as usual.

'This stuff is rubbish,' she said. 'I can't feel anything. I'm not getting any sensation whatsoever.'

I took a hit and knew instantly that she was right. 'This isn't touching me. It's brick dust.' I was getting angry. 'Let's go back to the pub and see the bloke that sold us this stuff. We've been had.'

Fergus had been in the kitchen, shooting up his smack. Walking into the front room he told me, 'Mine's all right, I got a good hit out of mine. When you smoke it, you lose a lot of the goodness. You need to be jacking it up, man, you need to be jacking it up.' He grinned. He meant injecting it.

So my next hit was through 'jacking up'. I watched, fascinated, as Fergus prepared the heroin so that it was ready for me to use. The 'rush' was fantastic, ten times more powerful than smoking it. A sensation of 'needles and pins' in my head and a tingling in my body seemed to increase the experience. The effect on my mind was as though I was caught up in a twilight state, just as though I was slipping into a deep sleep but not quite making it.

Every part of my mind and body had slowed right down.

I could hear Susanna retching but I wasn't able to help her. I couldn't move.

And from that point on, heroin was my master. It took over my life like a thief that I had invited in . . . and then would not leave. Every other aspect of my life paled into insignificance. My family, work, friends, even my own thoughts, took second, third, fourth place to my desire for heroin. I was totally hooked.

The strange thing was, I didn't think of myself as being addicted. But I was.

Susanna and I had a tempestuous relationship, regularly breaking up and not seeing each other for weeks. Then we'd meet at a pub or a squat and pick up where we had left off. We weren't passionately in love, but we both had a large appetite for drugs, and she was someone to share the experience with. So I suppose it was a relationship of convenience – and it *definitely* came second to drugs.

My need for heroin was growing daily. I went from jacking up at weekends to needing the drug Monday mornings just to feel 'normal'. At first, the hand of drug dependency gripped my mind and body for two days a week, then three, and it wasn't long before I needed smack *every day* just to get through it. And yet, I never saw myself as a junkie who was totally dependent on drugs to get through the week! I took regular baths, I looked after myself and thought that junkies were people who lived rough, looking unclean and dishevelled as they hunted around for their next fix. No; that was not me.

As my drug experimentation and dependency grew, I felt the need to be around my old friends. When

Susanna was off the scene, I wanted to feel as though I belonged somewhere. But when I attempted to visit my old mates, I found myself being shunned. Knocking on Dean's door one weekday evening I was told by his mum that he wasn't in. I had a strong feeling that he was, but that he didn't want to see me. I had the same reception at all my old mates' houses and, if I saw a friend in the street, they would either cross the road or walk past me. It was a terrible, hurtful and lonely time.

My perception of myself was blurred. I didn't see myself as others did. I thought of myself as the same as I'd always been: clean, clear-eyed, dependable, friendly. But that wasn't the Martyn the world saw. The truth was, nobody wanted to be associated with a loser, a junkie, a no-hoper – which I was.

I was able to keep my job going, which was a miracle, but as it wasn't a straightforward nine to five, my bad time-keeping went unnoticed. I had my own workshop and my boss was happy with me as long as I got the cars ready for when he needed them. But this was a barren, lost period in my life, one that was sucking me further and further down into the depths of human experience.

6

Addiction and Beyond

I knew I'd been turned over. Sitting in the squat on my own, the hours stretched out and I knew my 'friend' was not coming back with any drugs.

Not having drugs would trigger all sorts of fears, but the strongest one was about getting the next fix. As desperation began to kick in, I was trusting people I hardly knew to score for me. And now, weary, fed up and angry, I knew I'd been taken for a ride – again. But what was I supposed to do?

As I sat there alone, the hours crawling by, memories of my life only five years ago drifted into my mind. I was representing the school as an all-rounder athlete, healthy, strong, impatient to sample life as a young man – the whole world was before me. So, where had I gone wrong? I wanted to cry. The helplessness of my situation was overwhelming. Who cared about me? I couldn't turn to my parents; it would have destroyed them if they had found out what my life was really like. To them I was normal – I was working, eating and sleeping. What more could parents want? They had no idea . . . My old friends didn't want to associate with me; I had sunk too low even for them. I was caught up in an on-off relationship with Susanna, but the fact was that the foundation of our relationship was drugs, so it was doomed from the outset.

My outlook was bleak, and I had no one to blame but myself.

'How am I going to get myself out of this nightmare?'

Then suddenly I remembered someone – Peter. He had been my friend in school. We had both belonged to the athletic team and we'd made a formidable pair; no one could touch us in our chosen areas of sporting excellence. Peter's father ran the local church youth group, so every Wednesday evening we would go along to play pool, and have a chat there. Being part of this club was good for me at the time. I was able to socialise and meet up with other kids without the regimented rules of school. Peter and his family regularly attended church on a Sunday, and his dad would encourage youth club members to go as well; he also taught us about God and how to pray. Without realising, I had learnt a lot about the Bible – mainly stories like Adam and Eve, the Good Samaritan and the feeding of the 5,000 with five loaves and two fish. I liked praying, especially using the Lord's Prayer. The thought that I could speak to God, or just think about talking to Him and He'd hear me, was mind-blowing.

But would He hear me now, at my lowest point – a no-hoper, a junkie?

I had nothing to lose. So I clasped my hands together and called out to my friend Peter's God, asking Him to help me, and to get me out of this cesspit of drug dependency.

The next few days were a battle. I knew I needed to come off the drugs in order to get my life back, and maintain my sanity. But as soon as the cravings began to snake their way over my body and the yearning to inject myself grew, I put my good intentions off for another day. Then I tried a 'Do-it-yourself coming off heroin' programme, buying a bottle of methadone and some barbiturates.

Sitting on the settee in the lounge, I swallowed about 25 ml of the very sweet green liquid. It wasn't long before the aches and pains that come with withdrawal abated and I began to feel like myself. But, after a short time, the mental need for shooting up began to intensify. My need for heroin was strong, but the need to go through the physical motions – preparing the mixture for injecting, and then the injecting process itself – was stronger. I tried to stop myself from thinking about it, but it was impossible. I really needed to inject, *now*.

The barbiturate capsules lived in the sock drawer in my bedroom. I thought, 'If I just inject one capsule, perhaps that'll stop the mental anguish.' So I stuck the needle in my arm, and instantly passed out.

'Martyn, Martyn! Wake up, wake up, it's Dad!'

I felt as though I was floating somewhere out in space. I couldn't control my thoughts as they seemed separate from me. It was hard to control my body too. My dad was slapping my face, trying to get me to react. He was talking to me, expecting a reply. When I was able to stand up, he walked me up and down the length of the room, and my mum fed me black coffee. It took quite some time, but I managed to come round. They had found me with the syringe still hanging out of my arm.

Next morning my parents and I had a long talk. I told them all about my junkie life. They were shocked; shocked that I was living a desperate life and they hadn't realised. I was living in a world that was totally alien to them.

'Why, son? Why?' asked my mum.

I could see the pain and hurt in her face. Shame washed over me, and I wished I could erase all the terrible things I had done, just to please my mum and dad. But I couldn't.

'I knew you shouldn't have hung around with that girl!' Dad meant Susanna. My parents had never really liked her; they knew she enjoyed smoking and drinking . . . Now, they needed someone to blame, so Susanna took the brunt of their anger. But it wasn't her fault; it was *my* decision to get so deeply involved in drugs. Susanna was just someone I could get 'out of it' with.

My appointment with the GP resulted in my getting a further appointment at the Hackney Drug Dependency Unit. No more combing the streets and squats looking for shady dealers so I could score a hit! Now, I could just go to the Unit once a week, get my prescription, leave it at my local chemist, and daily pick up my bottle of methadone. My mind was still filled with the physical motions of injecting, but I knew that I'd been given a chance to break the habit, and I *had* to try; if I gave in, I would be addicted forever.

During one of the group sessions I had to attend, I linked up with a guy called Evan, who looked like a classic junkie, with matted greasy hair, five o'clock shadow and yellow teeth.

'Here's my address. Pop round and see me sometime.' He leaned closer and whispered, 'Got any methadone to sell?'

The methadone just about sustained me through the day. So, shaking my head, I said, 'No, I haven't got enough for myself, let alone to give away.'

He appeared to think for a moment and then said, 'You know you can get extra up in Harley Street?'

'Harley Street? What you talking about?'

'Devonshire Place, really, not Harley Street.'

Evan then explained about a doctor who gave out week-long prescriptions for physeptone ampoules, a heroin substitute, Ritalin, methadone linctus – and a bag of clean syringes and needles. It seemed like Christmas to me. Here I was, a habitual user of heroin, and I could be given everything I needed to stay on the drug, and all for about forty quid a week!

After I had obtained my first packet of drugs I gave Evan half, which I didn't mind, because I wouldn't have known about this doctor and her wonderful, cheap prescriptions if it hadn't been for him. From then on, I went halves with Susanna, £20 a week. And Susanna signed up with the doctor too.

My miracle-working doctor didn't question me too hard about my dependency.

'How are you this week, Mr Parrish?' she'd ask.

'Oh, not too good, Doctor. I've had a few problems at work that have pushed my stress levels right up.' I'd be lying, of course, but I didn't want to tell her I was fine, in case she discharged me and I was back to square one.

'Hmm. In that case, Mr Parrish, here's a prescription to last you for another week. Come and see me again.'

Sliding the forty quid across her desk, she in turn would hand me my repeat prescription. It was a good system. I was able to work out a method of getting extra drugs that were clean (with no fear of police intervention), along with sterile needles and syringes, more than I really needed, so I could sell half these drugs and, with that money, buy my drugs for the following week. I don't think this is what the doctors meant by drug-free – but to me, they were.

My life stabilised because my drug situation was stabilised. I was no longer thinking about giving up drugs as I could handle my life with the doctor's help. She was generous – she helped keep my drug addiction going for eight years.

Susanna and I decided that it made sense for us to live together. It was cheaper and less hassle when it came to our drug sharing. But I hadn't reckoned on her father.

'There's no way you're living with Susanna. It's either marriage or nothing.'

My parents were of the same mind.

Susanna's dad explained to us that if we got married he would help us financially but, if we lived together, we had to go it alone. Both Susanna and I were all for the financial help so we got married. Our parents organised everything: a white wedding in church, a Rolls-Royce, a sit-down meal for our guests . . . In between the church ceremony and the reception, Susanna and I had enough time to go back to the flat that my parents had given me a £2,000 deposit for, shoot up and get stoned. What seemed like an hour or so to us was in fact the best part of five or six hours. So by the time we got back, we only had about half an hour left of the party.

Married life was not good from the start. Susanna liked to party, I liked to stay at home. I tried, I *really* tried, with her. We struggled on in our relationship for a few years, but I could see that she lived for drugs and alcohol and I really wanted to tone down those areas of my life. I had tried unsuccessfully to stop taking drugs but, living with Susanna, who spent every waking minute either talking about drugs or taking them, made it impossible. I couldn't stop myself from giving in to temptation. And then, Susanna announced that she was pregnant.

For me, the whole concept of becoming a father was mind-boggling. All my life I'd had no one else to be concerned about, except myself. But now I was going to be totally responsible for another human being. When Susanna made her announcement, I knew deep in my heart that this was the push that I needed to completely finish the love affair that I had with drugs.

I had been injecting ten ampoules of physeptone – which was five mls of the drug – twice a day for the last few years. At first, trying to reduce my intake was a bit hit-and-miss; in my mind, I was determined, but my body was in rebellion. The fear of getting ill – withdrawal symptoms – was so great. I would try day after day to cut down until I was able to function with a lesser dose of the drug. Nights were the worst time, as I would experience agonising cramps in my legs and stomach. My legs would twitch and ache all night and the only way I could get comfortable was to either take some methadone or smoke some cannabis. Sometimes it felt like I was wasting my time and I might just as well get back on the gear full-time. But then I would think about my unborn son or daughter and say to myself: 'Who's going to look after the child? How can my child look up to me if I'm a junkie?' These thoughts would reinforce my willpower to be drug-free.

By the time my son was born, I was still using a little cannabis, but that was all. I'd had to constantly beg Susanna to stop taking drugs and drinking while she was pregnant, because I was so worried that the baby could be born with its own dependency. Thankfully, that wasn't the case.

Holding my son for the first time made me realise that all the physical problems I'd experienced in coming off the hard drugs were worth it. As he lay helplessly in my arms, I resolved in my heart that I was going to be a good and responsible father.

One morning, I took a good look at myself in the mirror. It was as though I was seeing myself for the first time. I was skin and bone, pale and insipid. My hair was lank and lifeless – I was a mess. I didn't feel good about myself inside or out. This was a huge awakening for me, and I knew I had to do something. So I joined a gym.

Regular exercise and good food began to change my shape. It also lifted my thoughts about myself – I'd had such low self-esteem – which made me begin to take more pride in my appearance.

My relationship with Susanna deteriorated rapidly after my son Scott was born. Now that I was drug-free, we drifted further apart. We were forever arguing, especially when she was drunk; the first couple of drinks would make her merry, happy and giggly but then she'd become argumentative and violent. When Scott was two years old, I had finally had enough and I left.

Leaving was like a huge weight lifting off my shoulders. It seemed as though I could breathe more easily. My greatest worry was that I had left Scott behind in Susanna's care. Her parents would have Scott most weekends and, because Susanna was living in a flat above her father's second-hand furniture shop, it was easy for her dad to regularly pop in to see them. I was working for Susanna's dad, and I enjoyed it, but I had to give the job up as Susanna kept coming down to the shop and hassling me.

I managed to get a job for a firm delivering industrial electric cables. I moved in with some friends and so my daily communication with Susanna was cut off. But I would visit her often, just to keep an eye on my son.

To not have to live a double life – working during the day and jacking up secretly in the evenings – was liberating. My life had become so insular and I hadn't even been aware of it. Now, though, I began to see my life more clearly. I was still smoking cannabis, but felt more in control of my life.

Leaving heroin behind meant that my friends had to go too – after all, most of them came through my long association with drugs. But through the gym, I met some doormen, and found out that gym regulars would spend time at the club where these doormen worked. I had not been looking for a girlfriend (I was a bit hesitant after Susanna!), but then Carol caught my eye. She taught aerobics at the gym and we became friends. I secretly fancied her but she was a beautiful woman, clean and decent, and I thought to myself, 'There's no way she'd be interested in me.' Still, we were now part of the same social circle, so it didn't seem odd when I monopolised her! Eventually, I plucked up the courage to ask her out. After that, we spent a lot of time together, spoke regularly on the phone, and I soon realised I was falling in love with her. And, as our relationship deepened, we decided that it would make more sense if we lived together.

Carol left the gym and became a veterinary nurse. I was still working as a delivery man, but to get some extra cash I was doing a bit of gardening. Then, one of the guys at the gym, a doorman, asked if I would do some door work. I had never thought about being a bouncer before, but when he told me how much I would get paid, I said yes.

I didn't know it at the time, but door work – and the people that I met through it – was to dramatically change my life.

7

The Good Life

When I went to pick up my wages, I was surprised to see that the owner of the security company that I had worked for was a guy I'd chatted to in a gym a few years back. He was a semi-professional bodybuilder named Ian McDowall. When he shook my hand, he said he remembered me, too. As he handed over my pay packet, I asked him if he had any more jobs going.

'Yeah, I have as it happens. I've got a couple of week-ends you can do.'

I was grateful and became quite involved with door work. Money was tight for me and Carol, so when Ian offered me some extra in the way of being a debt collector for his firm, I jumped at the chance. Most of the time I had to make an initial visit to a client concerning an unpaid bill and, once it was established how it was going to be settled, I would turn it over to Ian.

By now, my divorce from Susanna had become absolute. Carol and I had had a daughter, Katie, and moved from our home in Ilford to Chigwell. Scott was now spending weekends with Carol and me. We tried to make sure he was in a stable, safe, family environment and to let him know that what was happening in his own volatile home was unnatural – my son had phoned on quite a few occasions telling me how his mother and her then boyfriend were having drunken fights. I knew he was in danger, and the time came when we felt enough was enough, and decided to have Scott come to live with us. Susanna didn't contest my decision.

My relationship with Carol was marred by my paranoid insecurity. I knew she was completely different from Susanna but whenever she left for work I'd be imagining she was cheating on me. If she went to her works' Christmas party, or out for a night with her friends, again I would be fretting and getting worked up about what she might be doing. Obviously, this had a very negative effect on our relationship. It was in danger of crumbling, and I knew I had to do something about it.

Ian, my boss, was a Christian. I found I could really trust his word. He had proved this to me again and again. If he said he was going to do something, he would do it. What impressed me the most was when I told him that I had worked eight hours he never questioned it and he paid me accordingly, never trying to cheat me out of a penny. He didn't quibble over my hours or how much I earned; he paid me straight away. This was a new way of living to me – most people I knew would rob, lie and kill if they could get away with it, but not Ian.

Ian had a way about him that I admired; he was a gentleman. I liked the way he was with his wife and daughter and I liked the way he treated his employees. He earned great respect from everyone and no one crossed him. He was honest, truthful, kind and caring and yet still had a sense of humour. His whole way of handling himself in all sorts of situations – good, bad, volatile or humorous – always intrigued me. I wondered why more people couldn't be like him – starting with me! He had 'something' – which I now know to be 'Someone' – and I wanted to have what he had. He helped me overcome different insecurities and, as my confidence grew, so did my self-esteem. It was refreshing, after all the bad years that I had lived, to have someone who was willing to give me a chance and show me respect. So when he asked me if I would like to go to his church, I said yes.

Church and God had never really featured in my life – except for my time in the youth club, and my crying out to my friend Peter's God when I was at my lowest point. But I was willing to go to Ian's church, and that surprised me a bit. Still, I thought there had to be more to life than I'd experienced so far, and whether that had anything to do with 'God', I didn't know, but I reasoned that Ian was a Christian and the way he conducted himself and his life was because of his belief in God, so I couldn't see any harm in going to his church.

Ian's church was nothing like I'd expected, remembered or seen on TV's *Songs of Praise*. The people were trendy, modern and mostly young, with a few exceptions. There were families with young children who were able to roam about. Carol and I even let Katie go around introducing herself; we knew she was safe. Everyone was friendly, happy and had that certain 'something'. I reckoned it was worth going again just for the social side, although we also enjoyed the message – Pastor Sean O'Boyle was so funny and entertaining. I just listened, soaking it all up.

'. . . I turned away from the violence that was so much a part of my job. I didn't want to injure anyone and I didn't want to be hurt myself. Since Jesus has come into my life, my outlook, what is important and what isn't, has changed. I want to live the rest of my life for the Lord Jesus.'

Sitting at the back of a theatre in Clacton-on-Sea, Carol and I listened to Tough Talk, speaking to a lot of people about Jesus. I suppose I'd thought Christians in general were nerdy, geeks. But these guys – Arthur, Steve and Ian – had muscles popping out all over the place. As they recounted their lives, I was shocked. They had been through some terrible things, and yet here they were, bold as brass, talking about God. It was mind-boggling.

One day, when I'd dropped into the office to get my wages, Ian had asked me if I'd like to come to a meeting he was holding. To start with, I had mixed feelings about attending, but I was glad that I did! On the way home, Carol and I talked non-stop about what had been said.

'Martyn, how do those guys know that God has forgiven them? And what about the people they hurt or abused – what can God do for them?'

'I have no idea. Those guys don't look like Christians to me. If it wasn't for the fact that I work for Ian and I kind of know him, I'd say people only become Christians to get out of bad situations . . . or to appease their conscience.'

'But they seemed genuine. They really believe in the Bible.'

I knew I needed some answers. So, at work, I picked up a Bible that was on a shelf in the office and began to read it. I didn't really know where to start, but I plunged in. My reading skills hadn't been up to much when I was younger, but now I found Luke's Gospel came alive, and I could see from the pages that Jesus was a powerful man. I believed that Jesus did exist, but was He the Son of God? Perhaps He was some guy who had power to heal sick people and multiply food. But where did that leave me? What could He do to help the likes of me?

For the next few months, I pondered what the Bible said and how it could apply to my life. But I can honestly say that working with Ian, watching the way he behaved, *that* was what impressed me about Christianity.

One day, when I came back to work after a holiday, Ian called me into his office. I was expecting him to offer me another door job, so I was quite surprised when he said, 'Martyn, would you like to work here in the office as an operational manager?' I was very surprised. Not long ago I was injecting myself with drugs, and then my life turned completely around – and now this! I counted myself very lucky. I accepted and soon I was working alongside Ian and his wife Valerie managing their door security operations, organising the shifts, dealing with managers of premises or companies. I loved it – and it was a good opportunity to get answers to some of the questions I had about the Bible.

'Eh, Ian, do you think that Jesus really walked on water? I mean, after all, He was only a bloke.'

He laughed. 'Yes, He's Jesus, after all.'

Slowly, I came to see that Christianity is for everyone – you just needed faith and to believe the Bible. Every day I would think about Jesus. Being able to know Jesus *personally*, even though you couldn't see Him physically, was very intriguing. It felt as though I was coming alive to the prospect of knowing Jesus for myself. It was incredible to think that an ex-junkie who had done bad things could be forgiven, everything forgotten, and could literally be a new person.

During this time, I had not been feeling quite myself. I'd been getting stomach cramps and sometimes the pain was unbearable. I was still working and looking after my family, trying not to pay too much attention to what was happening to my body; when the pain came, I would just have a hot bath and the heat would soothe away the discomfort. Then, one day, the pain greatly intensified and I was in agony. For ten days I was in constant pain and no amount of hot baths could help. My doctor told me it was Irritable Bowel Syndrome and gave me some medicine, but the pain became so bad that I had to go to Casualty at my local hospital. A doctor came to see me and he couldn't work out what was wrong. It took a few more doctors to try and take some blood from me for tests, but none of them could locate a vein. The years of jacking up had taken its toll on my body. Fortunately, the surgeon on call that day was a bowel specialist who took one look at me and said: 'This man has got to go to theatre, *now*.' And pandemonium broke out as doctors and nurses rushed around, preparing me for surgery.

I woke up at seven o'clock the next morning with a large surgical plaster across my stomach, a drip in one arm and a colostomy bag. For seven days, I thought I had bowel cancer and was going to die. My fear was that I would not see my son and daughter grow up and have families of their own. I couldn't believe that my life was abruptly coming to an end. I asked Carol to bring my Bible so that I could read it. The words brought comfort to me and I asked the Lord if He could help me out of this situation. My family needed me – it just wasn't the right time to leave them. As I read the Bible, I found myself discovering truths that I hadn't previously 'seen' and I knew that something was happening to my heart.

I was diagnosed with diverticulitis and was told that if I had not been operated on soon after I had been admitted to hospital, I would be dead. The surgeon said my bowel had burst about ten days before I was admitted and he was totally amazed that I was able to walk around without collapsing.

Throughout my ordeal, the church that Carol and I had been attending infrequently had been praying for me; the pastor and Ian and other Christians had been praying that I would be healed. And I was. I came home and returned to work very soon. But after six months, the colostomy was bothering me; I wanted it reversed. The surgeon told me that the waiting list was at least six months to a year but I couldn't wait that long. Then he informed me that he worked in the Casualty department a few days a month and if I happened to turn up, in pain, on the day he was working . . . *Fortunately*, the day I went to Casualty *happened* to be the day he was working. I got my reversal.

I was happy. My health was good, I had a regular job and, soon after my reversal, Carol told me she was pregnant again. It was like the icing on the cake. I would be around for my children, and now I going to be a dad again!

When Adam was three months old, we moved to Buckhurst Hill in Essex. We now lived in a house with a garden, ideal for my children. Carol had been taking Adam to a local church to attend a Mother and Toddlers group. Here she met Ruth Dronsfield, whose son was in our daughter's class at school. Ruth and Carol became friends and, one day as they both walked the children to school, Carol told Ruth that she had gone to church that weekend, and Ruth told Carol she was a Christian. (I should have known that Ruth was a Christian as she had that special 'something' just like Ian! They both had Jesus in their lives – I know that now.)

I was pleased that Carol had a friend who knew the Lord. I had Ian to help me understand Christianity, but Carol had had no one. One day, Carol told me that she had been feeling ill earlier in the day and Ruth had prayed for her; as Ruth had prayed, she said it seemed as though her 'heart was warmed'. Previously, she had believed that there was a God, but that He wasn't interested in her. Now, she believed that somehow God had poured His love into her, and she was changed.

I was glad. I hadn't told Carol that I had been reading my Bible as often as I was. I was getting hooked on reading it and wanted to know more about God. I hadn't known how to break this to Carol and was fearful of ridicule. Now, we decided that as we both wanted to know more about Jesus, we were prepared to put past hurts and problems behind us, and move forward. I began to find that the more I read my Bible the more I found answers to my everyday life. Situations that had perplexed me would be solved as I read God's Word and prayed, handing all my anxieties over to Him. Usually I would have either worried about it all or tried to sort it out myself, but now I really felt that God was looking after me. In fact, when I looked back on my life from my schooldays, particularly as an athlete, and in my early working life and drug abuse years, I could see that God had been watching over me all the time.

The motorcycle accidents that I had, resulting in broken bones, damaged vehicles, near misses but no huge major accidents in which anyone died – that was God.

Thinking about my drug years, especially when I injected anything that was remotely like drugs into my body and still lived – that was God.

How Susanna was able to get pregnant with Scott, because of our chronic drug dependency, and that he was born with no dependency – that was God. Scott was a blessing from the Lord. He didn't become a dysfunctional teenager and he has turned out to be a well-adjusted young man. And, even though he doesn't realise it yet – that was God.

Meeting Carol – that was God. My daughter's birth brought it home to me that I was very privileged to become a dad. It cemented my relationship with Carol, causing us to have a closeness that I had never truly experienced with another person – that was God.

Meeting Ian – that was God.

Having a burst bowel would have killed most people yet I survived, to the astonishment of the medical profession – that was God.

The Lord had been working His way into my life and Carol's individually, and this had drawn us even closer together. Reading God's Word clearly showed how we should be living and, as yet, Carol and I were not married. We realised that if we wanted to move on and mature in Jesus we would have to tie the knot. So we did.

Ian and his wife Valerie helped organise and pay for our wedding. I felt a bit embarrassed that he wanted to help us in this way but, during the time that I had got to know Ian, I'd come to realise that giving is a strong Christian trait. He was just doing what was in his heart.

The wedding day was great. Our friends and family came and it seemed to me as though I was caught up in a dream. And this time, I really meant my wedding vows.

And now . . .

Within a year of getting married, Carol and I were baptised. We had been regularly attending the Vineyard Church in Loughton, Essex. Through Carol's friendship with Ruth and her husband David, we had been nurtured and encouraged as new Christians. (Caroline and Ben Matatia also helped enormously with our baptism course.) The baptism was a public declaration of what we believed and, for me, it was important that people knew who I was *now*.

Since I became a Christian, my friend Ian has been supportive in helping me grow in my faith. At the time of being 'introduced' to Jesus, it was his manner, his honesty and concern that made me think, 'If he's a Christian and that's how he behaves, I would like to be like that, too.' It wasn't so much what Ian said, it was more what he did that spoke volumes to me. He was 'walking the walk' and that had a more profound effect on me than 'talking the talk'.

If I had never got to know Ian, I would never have become so involved in Christian ministry, and I wouldn't be having such a good life in Jesus. Jesus has made me new in my heart, in my thoughts, and in my everyday walk with Him. Many of my junkie friends are either dead or dying but I am alive and well and have a family that loves me, and I them. There are people around that care about me, and are interested in my life. All this can only be down to Jesus!

SIMON
PINCHBECK

1

The Pain in Spain

'C'mon, Simon! We'd better make a run for it.' Lynda, my wife, forged ahead through the crowd of people. The airport was packed. Dodging around holidaymakers with their children was not fun.

Quickly, we showed our documents to the stewards and headed for the plane. My mind was churning over with many different thoughts – many of them murderous. The journey was uneventful, but what was happening inside of me was *bad*. My wife didn't know it, but we were not going on holiday for a week of relaxation. I was on a mission. I had been ripped off and I was going to Spain to get my money back – all £100,000 of it.

Our hotel was surrounded by landscaped gardens and our room was overlooking the sea. It was paradise.

'Thanks, love, for this.' My wife pecked me on the cheek and smiled. 'This is just what the doctor ordered.'

I sipped my Scotch and gritted my teeth. I could feel the fire of anger inside me. I felt like crushing the glass in my hand and smashing it into someone's face.

'Simon?' Lynda looked at me. 'You sure you're OK?'

'Yeah, I'm fine, sweetheart. Honest.'

It was easy to lie to my wife. Lying had become second nature to me, especially now. If she really knew why I had brought her to Spain it would have been another nail in my coffin. My marriage was already in a very precarious position.

I turned away from her. Taking the card out of my pocket, I looked again at the details on it. This was the link for me to get my money back. Every time that figure – £100,000 – appeared in my mind, I wanted to kill. The guy that I had been introduced to in England, Vic, had enticed me into his scheme – a scheme that was going to set me up for life. I'd been warned about him and the other guys; that they were dangerous, they had top connections, they were ruthless – but through them you could earn *proper* money.

It was the 'proper money' bit that had me hooked. I loved money. In fact, I would go as far as to say that I *worshipped* money; it was my god. I can't remember when I first had a deep yearning for money, but the need and hunger for it was fixed deep within me. My biggest fear, one that I'd had all my life, was that I would never have any. For the last few years, I had been able to get my hands on more money then I could ever have earned as a copper. But now, this deal that I was involved in seemed rotten through and through.

Since my retirement as a police constable, my life has gone from one extreme to another. When I'd stepped out of the station for the last time, I'd felt free. A cloak of heaviness had been lifted off my shoulders and now I could pursue my dreams. I wanted to be self-employed, my own boss. I wanted my family to live in a nice area with a big house and swimming pool. I wanted the biggest and flashiest cars. I wanted to eat in the best restaurants, wear the fanciest clothes and, whatever my heart desired, I wanted to know that I could buy it. And I'd do anything to make my dreams a reality.

At the poolside, I couldn't relax. My whole body was tense. It was taking all my willpower to sit on the sun-lounger. Standing up, I stretched out my six foot four inch frame, flexed my muscles and said to Lynda, 'I'm gonna check up on the lads at home and make a few phone calls. All right, love?'

Up in our room, I rang the number on the card a few times. Each time I was getting a Spanish bloke who couldn't speak of word of English. Slamming the phone down, I knew I had to do more than just sit in this room. I went downstairs, hailed a taxi from outside the hotel, and watched the Spanish countryside whiz past.

I reached my destination, knowing my money was *somewhere* in this town. I stalked through the streets, bumping and crashing into people. I didn't care whether I hurt them or not. Thrusting the card with the details on it into people's faces only brought me negative reaction. I was wild by this time. A guy walked past me and I grabbed his arm, holding out the card for him to read.

'Do you know this place?'

He seemed a bit scared and shrugged his shoulders. I let him go. Walking away, he turned and smirked at me. In that instant, I snapped. I rushed at him, swung him round by his shoulder, nearly lifting him off the ground, and flung him across some tables and chairs outside a restaurant. People screamed.

'Where is he?' I yelled. 'Where's the man with my £100,000? I know he's here somewhere!'

Sweat was rolling off my face, blinding my eyes. Looking up at the sky I thought to myself, 'If there is a god, please help me to get my money!' It was hypocrisy, but I was willing to try *anything* to get my nest egg back.

Over the next few days, I walked and walked, circled the marinas, asked a thousand questions and no one could help me. At last, I was confronted with the horrible truth. I'd been carved up badly and my money was gone – forever.

Back at the hotel, I looked at myself in the mirror and didn't like what I saw. It wasn't my physical features that were upsetting me, it was the stark truth that I had been lied to, cheated on, and deceived. Not by the strangers I was seeking in Spain, but by my so-called mates and business partners. They had purposely sent me on a wild goose chase, and all the time they knew full well where my money was. Probably shared out amongst them! I imagined that they were laughing at me – a copper taken for a ride. Who could I complain to – the police? I had been taken for a mug!

What these criminal acquaintances of mine did not know was that they had destroyed my dream of 'having it all'. Because I had really bought into this dream, I had loads of credit cards and had run up huge amounts of debt. I'd believed this latest deal would mean cracking open a treasure trove of endless cash, so I'd been careless and gone on a spending spree . . . on borrowed money.

Emotions were churning inside me. I really should have given myself time to think about plunging all my money into the project. I remembered times when I would be discussing the deal with a few of my 'mates' and one would give the other a sidelong glance, or something was said that caused me to feel a 'check', a little twinge of doubt. But I'd been greedy, thinking how much I'd make out of my investment. And now it was all gone.

I felt the need to settle the matter, preferably by slowly killing each man involved. But there was a problem. If I'd had to deal with these guys on a one-to-one basis, I could have, but I knew the reality of the situation – the only way I could deal with these men would be as a group. I also knew for sure that I would probably end up missing for weeks and, when I was found, it would be in a shallow grave in Epping Forest or as food for the pigs.

'What a fool you've been, Simon,' I muttered to myself. 'What a fool!'

2

Young Days

'C'mon, you Rams!'

I was yelling at the top of my voice for Derby County, my local club. I loved football, not that I was much of a player myself – rugby was my game – but I revelled in the whole atmosphere of a football match: the jeering, the cheering, the baiting of the opposition and the adrenaline rush when your team scored a goal; all of this made Saturday afternoon something to look forward to. And then there was the drinking and the guaranteed fighting afterwards. At sixteen, I was very tall for my age and no one ever questioned me, so I could go in the pub and drink as much as I liked.

One time, pushing my way through the thick bodies of football fans, I was eager to down my fifth pint of the day. Just as I reached the bar, a mighty roar went up. Even before I turned round, I knew what was happening. The opposition had come into the pub. All thoughts of a pint were gone as windows were smashed, tables overturned, and a mass exodus of Derby boys tried to get through the doors.

'C'mon, lads! Let's get the Forest scum!'

It was fantastic. Once out on the street I would be swinging my fists, hollering for blood and trying to do as much damage to people as possible before the sirens came wailing down the street. Little did I know that one day I would be one of the dreaded 'filth'.

As I said, I wasn't a footballer. I had the right physique to be a rugby player and I was always a member of the first team at school. Before every match I would psych myself up by thinking of some of the football skirmishes I had been involved with and, by the time I got on the pitch, I was ready for a battle. Stomping out to the playing field I was *angry*, and the only way to be relieved would be to kick a few heads and to make sure that we won. And kick heads I did; once, the opposing team's star player was tackled and went down. He was shielding the ball, and my boot came down hard on his face. He screamed as the studs pierced his skin. He was stretchered off, and we went on to win the game.

Apart from that sort of action, living in Burton-on-Trent as a teenager in the mid 1970s was mundane. From a very early age, I wanted to be a millionaire. I didn't really know how I was going to achieve this, but I planned to earn as much as I could by the time I was twenty-one. From the age of fourteen, I began running scams. My local boozer allowed underage drinking and it was there that I was able to do my wheeling and dealing. I knew a bloke who had his fingers in lots of pies; one day, he showed me his car boot, stuffed with black bags. Rummaging around, I found some sports shirts and tracksuits, and knocked all the stuff out at school, at the rugby club and down the pub. I was good at selling and was able to build up a clientele who would put in for orders.

My parents were totally unaware of my clandestine operations. My dad was a salesman, forever striving to make more money; it never happened while I was living at home, but years later, he did manage to make a few bob. Mum was a nurse and she worked very hard for my brother, sister and me. I knew how my parents struggled, so I never put any pressure on them where money was concerned. I sorted myself out, and was able to keep myself in the latest fashions, drink and whatever else I needed. But all the time I knew there was *more*, and I wanted it.

One summer, I got a job in a slaughterhouse, earning £100 a week. It was a fortune, and every penny was mine. I had loads of mates and would stand a round, making sure everyone had something to drink. Alcohol was a big part of my life, girls were second. I loved weekends, and from Friday night until Sunday I was out discoing, drinking and womanising – and having the occasional fight.

My parents were adamant that I stayed on at school because they felt that education was the way for me to better myself, and get a good job. But I nearly missed out on the sixth form because of my love of booze. I was regularly going to the pub during school lunchtime, but I got caught during one of my lunchtime sessions. The headmaster didn't want me back – he said I was a 'bad example' – and my dad was livid. His hand was shaking when he read the letter.

'Simon, what have you done?' He waved the letter in my face. 'You stupid idiot! Don't you realise you're blowing your whole future away? You've *got* to go back.'

'I don't want to go back. I want to make money.'

'Money, money! That's all you want, money! You are going back to school whether you like it or not. You are going to study for two more years and you are going to make something of your life.' He pointed his finger at me and said something that came back to haunt me years later. 'Having lots of money isn't all it's cracked up to be. Believe me, it will be your *downfall*!'

Because of my dad's pleading, I was allowed to take my place in the sixth form. But life for me went on as usual. The slaughterhouse job was gone and, with it, the £100. Having had a taste of money, I craved more. I was shifting loads of gear but I never seemed to have enough cash; the trouble was, the flipside of my desire to earn was to spend it just as quickly. This, in turn, made the urge to have money grow stronger and stronger. It was as though I was enslaved in the pursuit of getting as much money as I could, only to let it slip through my fingers like water. But it was a wonderful feeling, being able to treat my friends to drinks, and having money was a definite girl-puller. I had a string of girls eager to be with me as I was 'Mr Spender'.

I still played rugby for the school, but now I was also playing for the local club too. I was quite well known in Burton-on-Trent; wherever I went, I was usually recognised, either for my skills as an entrepreneur or for my over-indulgence in alcohol or for my rugby tackling skills or for my two-timing . . . never for my academic qualities. The truth was, by the time I was eighteen, I felt I had lived life to the full. Burton-on-Trent was too small and I knew that I needed to spread my wings if I was ever going to fulfil my ambition to become mega-rich. My only problem was, 'Where do I go from here?'

The answer came through my careers officer. I didn't really want to see him as I thought he would not be able to advise me on how to make a lot of money. As he was droning on, during the interview, I imagined saying to him, 'Sir, can you give me advice on how I open up a strip club and an illegal gambling den, and earn myself a million pounds?' But I soon snapped out of my daydreams when he said something about the police force.

'Police force? Never gave it a thought.'

'You should, lad, you should. Big strapping lad like you could really make your mark in a career like that. What do you think?' He handed me some leaflets. I took them, stashed them away, and quickly forgot all about them.

Then, a few days later, I was parked in front of the television, glued to the latest episode of *The Sweeney*. It was my favourite programme and I loved the way it portrayed policing, London-style. The car chases, taking on hardened criminals, lots of violence, pulling the birds – and, of course, the endless drinking. The Flying Squad – these were my kind of coppers!

That night, as I was getting my holdall ready for school the next day, the leaflets fell out. I read them avidly. Scenes from *The Sweeney* flashed through my mind. I was there, on my two-way radio as the car sped through red lights, hot on the tail of the bad guys . . . I nodded my head.

'Yeah. This police business, it could just be the right thing for me.'

I didn't see myself in a uniform. I was in plain clothes, Mr Cool, good cop, bad cop, invincible. But not in Staffordshire. It had to be the Met!

3

Finding My Feet (With My Fists!)

'Attention! Class fall in!' ordered the drill sergeant.

Standing ram-rod straight, I thought to myself, 'Here we go again.'

It was the fifth week of my police training at Hendon College. I hated it. My life had radically changed since I had had my 'brainwave' and joined the police. It was absolutely nothing like I had envisaged. I wanted to go from base camp to *The Sweeney*. All the rules and regulations – it was terrible! At home, I was master of my own time. I could do what I wanted when I wanted, and even my parents mostly left me alone. Here, it seemed as though I couldn't even *yawn* without someone telling me it was wrong and I would be in trouble!

August was the wrong month for me to be banged up inside a hot stuffy classroom learning about police techniques and procedures. Often, I would spend the time daydreaming about the life I had left behind – the drinking, the scams, the girls, and just having a good time . . . why had I wanted to leave?

'Pinchbeck, are you still with us?' barked the lecturer, as my classmates sniggered.

Switching back to reality was painful at times and I wanted out. Yet, there was *something* that compelled me to keep going. Then, one evening, I was watching the *News*. The Notting Hill Carnival was in full swing and I saw the police with their batons and shields running around keeping order. I realised, 'Yeah, this *is* what I want to do.' I wanted to get in on the action.

The four months of training slowly crept by and finally I was assigned to Holloway Police Station. What a culture shock!

The area covered Finsbury Park, Highbury, Holloway, Archway and Tufnell Park – not the most pleasant parts of London (to me, anyway). I had never seen tenement ghetto-type council flats until I worked that beat. Many of the people who lived there were living below the poverty line. It was a melting pot of people from all around the world and, quite frankly, I was not prepared for it.

As I walked the streets of north London, the same look of despair and desperation seemed to haunt the eyes of adults and children alike. I found it overwhelming – and I could not see how working in this environment could get me to the level I wanted to be. It would be two whole years of pounding the beat, dealing with people who I very quickly thought of as lowlife, before I could hope to taste the pleasures of being in the CID.

In Burton-on-Trent, I was somebody. People knew me for many different reasons. I was a recognisable figure. In Holloway, I was desperate to attain that same status, to fill the void and overcome the feel of being a nonentity. But what could I do? The answer came very soon.

It was a late afternoon and I had only been on duty for an hour or so. I was thinking about how I could get myself out of this boring rut, when a voice blared out from the radio attached to my jacket.

'Assistance, urgent assistance!' The voice gave the name of a road, and my heart began to thud as I realised I wasn't very far away. So I shouted, '177, just round the corner,' and raced up the street. As I rounded the corner, I saw one of my colleagues struggling with two youths. The policeman had hold of one of them, whilst the other one was trying to prise his mate free.

I just ploughed into the first youth and knocked him to the ground with a nicely timed right hook. His mate, already on the ground, tried to scramble away, but a deft boot to the ribs rendered him powerless. Clipping on the handcuffs, I felt as though I had just had a bit part in *The Sweeney*! To be honest, although it was all over in seconds, I could have gone on. This was like old times at a football match, booting the opposition, or outside the pub tackling the enemy, giving them a good beating. It was great.

A police van pulled to the kerb. The sergeant jumped out and said, 'Well done, lads.'

The guy that I had helped replied, 'No, Sarge, it was nothing to do with me. It was all Pinchy's work. He came round the corner like Superman and, next thing I knew, they were both on the deck. It was amazing!'

Little did I know, but this was the start of my new life and reputation. Over the next few months, whenever there was a bit of trouble and muscle was needed, I was the man for the job. Any aggravation, Pinchy was summoned. I would knock a few heads, boot a few bodies and generally sort things out. Soon I came to the attention of the high-ranking officers. I knew they respected me because of my fearless approach in dealing with violent criminals. I was loved by my peers, and hated by the villains.

The only fly in the ointment was that deep down I still hankered after the big bucks. I knew that a working policeman was not going to wind up a multimillionaire, or even a millionaire for that matter. How could I hit the big time? I used to dream about running a bar in Spain, or perhaps owning a couple of nightclubs in London, or a five-star restaurant. I even considered buying a greyhound or horse, anything to generate serious money.

I knew even then there was an emptiness inside of me. I tried to push it away so I didn't have to acknowledge it, but when I did, I convinced myself that it was there because I was not living the rich life I felt I should living. I always thought there was something better for me. I reasoned that I would have to keep searching until I found it.

My fists enabled me to become the Heavyweight Boxing Champion of the Police Force in 1982. My rugby skills also enhanced my reputation and it became a pleasure to go to work. I loved walking through the police station to calls of 'All right, Pinchy?', 'Here's the nutter!' and 'Have you taken your medication?' The familiarity, the praises, the camaraderie and the adoration boosted my ego and increased my kudos. My drinking increased, partly because the beer in London was half the strength of what I was used to, and so, to get the same boozy effect, I had to drink more. But I never correctly gauged my intake and drank far too much.

Walking around the pitch at Highbury for the first time was a spine-tingling moment. I had seen the stadium on the telly, but to actually be there in person (and for free) was heady stuff. Football duty was where I *really* lived up to my reputation. When the match was on, my eyes would roam the terraces, seeking out potential troublemakers. I'd be fired up, ready to charge into battle. It was a great way for me to unleash my aggression, stomping on bodies, bashing heads and keeping order.

My colleagues loved having me around. It created a strong sense of brotherhood – we were shoulder to shoulder against the enemy.

After a period of time, I began to develop an affinity with the Arsenal fans. They were sort of like good friends. Whenever an Arsenal fan was in physical conflict with the opposition, no matter who was at fault, I would always side with the Arsenal guy.

Many of the policemen wore moustaches and I followed suit. I stood out as my moustache was long and bushy, and the Arsenal fans nicknamed me 'The Walrus'. When I was on duty at Highbury, the supporters would shout out from the terraces: 'Watch out, it's The Walrus!' I felt like a film star.

It was a cold, wintry afternoon when a big fight broke out on the terraces. It was a Spurs versus Arsenal match and I could sense the animosity in the air. Bracing myself for a violent confrontation, I waded in with the rest of my police mates, giving the Spurs fans particular attention. One of the Spurs supporters was at the front, gesturing with his fists, so I grabbed him by the neck and, holding him in a head lock, led him on parade in front of the Arsenal fans. The chant went up, 'Arsenal Old Bill, Arsenal Old Bill!' and I smiled at them, giving the thumbs-up sign as the cheers got louder.

As the violence escalated, I became hardened and cynical. There was no place in my life for weakness and sympathy. I wanted to end all situations with my fists; I would hit first and ask questions later. My vulnerability as a human being was not something I ever thought about – until one day when I nearly lost my life.

Arsenal was playing at home to West Ham. There was lots of chanting, swearing and an almost tangible feeling of violence filled the air. I was psyched up and ready to get into the thick of the fray I knew was soon coming. And come it did.

A loud roar went up and the two sides began a deadly combat as arms and legs dealt blow after blow. My colleagues and I waded in, eager to clobber a few bodies. Suddenly, on the other side of the Arsenal hardcore supporters, an enormous red flare flashed into the air. My eyes were dazzled, and a surge of West Ham fans attacked the Arsenal supporters in a cleverly orchestrated ambush.

I charged into the middle of the red smoke. I automatically assumed that my colleagues were behind, so with great confidence, I forged ahead. But then I realised, to my horror, I was completely alone – not one of my squad was with me.

Both sets of supporters turned their evil, violent attention on me. I was surrounded by angry, contorted faces, with teeth bared and fists poised, ready to attack. I knew they wanted my blood. I whipped off my helmet and held it firmly in one hand, gripping my truncheon in the other. In a split second, both sides pounced on me like hungry lions trying to topple their prey. I feared for my life. I was alone with the enemy baying for my blood, and I realised that if I fell to the ground then my life would be over. I would be beaten and trampled to death, with no mercy.

It seemed like ages before the cavalry arrived. I felt faint and weak but there was no way that I was going to reveal that I was *really* scared, for the first time in my life. Some sort of order was restored – although after the match, there was chaos in the streets and one young man did lose his life. It could so easily have been me.

Later, in the pub, nobody would ever have known what was going on inside of me. I was laughing and joking with my police colleagues about the match and how we dealt with the football supporters. But, that night, as I lay on my bed, horrible thoughts crashed through my mind as I relived the moment when I thought I was going to be overpowered, killed. I was so *alone* at that moment. The sickening reality dawned on me – I wasn't Superman or any other hero. I was a mere, mortal man. And it was sobering.

Lynda was the icing on the cake for me at that time in my life. Slim, blonde, smart, funny, independent, with a strong sense of responsibility, she was different from most of the other girls I had met. It wasn't long before I found myself standing in church saying my vows to her. Her dad was a police inspector, so she was familiar with police life.

We started our married life in a police house in Finchley, north London. Not far away from where we lived was a place called The Bishops Avenue. The enormous houses in this road are straight out of a fairy tale, with long, sweeping drives, Mercedes and Rollers parked out front, tall trees dotted along the way . . . and high security gates to keep the riff-raff out.

I would often jog slowly down this road, glancing from left to right at the vast display of wealth these houses represented. 'One day,' I would say to myself, 'I will own one of these.' I imagined myself ensconced in palatial splendour, perhaps with a servant or two.

My life was never boring. Every shift brought something different. Holloway, being the area it was, had many characters that were fearless and violent and it was part of my job to subdue and arrest. A well-known criminal who had caused untold grief to the area was seen coming out of somewhere he shouldn't have been. He became very violent, and the officers who were dealing with him were having a difficult time. Then I stepped in. He was handcuffed and installed in the van – no problem! However, his appearance at court was such that the magistrate commented on his heavily bruised face.

So, my name was synonymous with 'fearless copper' – tough nut, nutcase, enforcer. Someone who wasn't afraid of bending the rules. The funny thing was, I wasn't quite satisfied. I had all that a man could want in his life at that time, but I secretly wanted more. I aspired to the Flying Squad; I yearned to be promoted to that elite group. I remembered seeing a well-known villain being brought into the station, a man whose name was linked with armed robberies; he was still wearing a stocking over his face, and he looked menacing. The plain clothes guys who'd escorted him through the doors looked as though they had just come from filming the latest episode of *The Sweeney*. The Flying Squad carried guns, baseball bats, pickaxe handles, and had handcuffs dangling from their waistbands. They placed the weaponry on the station officer's desk; the atmosphere was filled with controlled aggression. This was what I wanted. But I was offered a post in the Crime Squad. Well, I reckoned, that would do me for now – the Crime Squad was the next best thing.

4

Change

I worked hard and played even harder. It was one massive round of early morning raids, kicking in doors, searching houses for contraband, targeting local villains and giving them a proper shake-up, letting them know who was boss.

I was in court giving evidence twice or more times a week. I was an expert in the witness box and my evidence was always clear and concise. I had to swear on the Bible that the evidence I was giving was true. The Bible had no meaning to me whatsoever; it could have been a copy of *Woman's Weekly*, it was irrelevant.

After my colleagues and I had had a good nick, we would go down the local pub and knock back as many pints as we could – which was usually a lot – followed by a Greek or Turkish meal to soak up the booze.

My time in the Crime Squad was further enhanced by the fact that we had no one looking over our shoulders, telling us what we could or could not do. And the senior officers were very pleased with the unit because we were getting the results that made politicians happy. As for me, I had it all worked out: the Crime Squad; CID; the Flying Squad. I didn't have much time for my wife.

We were like ships passing in the night. I didn't have the time or the inclination to ask her how she was feeling, or if she was happy. As long as I was pursuing my dreams, striving to get to the next level, to fill the void in my life, I didn't see the need to deepen the relationship.

The early eighties saw social unrest in London, which triggered the Brixton riots. It seemed to be kicking off throughout the region and the police were alerted to the possibility of large-scale violence erupting in the streets. One day, our chief inspector came into our unit to inform some of us that we would be leaving the Crime Squad 'to form a special unit whose primary job is to quell any violent disorder in Holloway before it happens'. When my name was called, I was ecstatic.

The Divisional Support Squad was made up of ten of my colleagues and me. We had no sergeant, there was just us to take care of any hint of violent uprising, and to stamp it out. We would tour the streets, stopping groups of youths who had congregated on the street corners looking for trouble – they found it in our unit. We would round them up and take them to the station. They quickly got the message and as soon as they saw our van, they disappeared like mist. It was definitely kicking off in Stoke Newington and Hackney, so our team would drive into the area without any authorisation and get stuck in, helping the locals sort out the rebels. It was proper policing as far as I was concerned. This was why I had joined up – to be part of the action.

The DS unit was so successful that it was made into a more organised and official unit. The numbers swelled; sergeants and inspectors were added and we had a proper shift rota. We used to take out suspects that had knives, guns and vicious implements. We were properly trained and briefed. Then the balloon burst and things radically changed.

Two black youths were picked up by members of the DS squad, held in the van and, apparently, assaulted. Then an urgent call was received by these members, they stopped the van, and released the young men. Then they drove off. The young guys were angry, and told their stories to their legal representatives. Consequently, the members of the DS unit were witch-hunted to find the culprits. But, although even top policemen thought *my* hands were all over the incident, they were wrong. Those involved in this case were found, charged, found guilty and imprisoned. However, this really made me think. I'd been involved in numerous incidents, many of them worse than this; any one of them could have ended in the same way. It all shook me up so much I came to the conclusion that I had to change my style of policing. A job came up in Crouch Hill as a Community Officer and I jumped at it. I thought I should keep a low profile for a while.

'Pinchbeck, you're just the man to sort out the youths on these estates and get some kind of order back.'

Nodding, I agreed with the chief inspector. I wanted a bit of an easy ride, time to get my head together, and see where I needed to be heading. I thought to myself, 'Get yourself established on the estates, knock a few heads together, sort out the troublemakers in your usual fashion . . . ' But would the chief inspector, or my colleagues, back me up? Judging by the way in which my name was called into question about the incident with the youths in the van, I wasn't so sure. So I decided I'd handle things differently.

On the estates, I quickly rounded up the leaders of the gangs. Many of them were hardcore Arsenal supporters and knew me, so it was straightforward.

'Listen, guys,' I said. 'Don't cause trouble on your own doorstep, or I will have to deal with you, and you don't want that, right?'

'OK, Walrus,' nodded a guy with a tattooed face. 'We get the picture.'

And so, the gangs conducted their criminal activities far from home, and I was able to do my job with the least aggravation. The high-ranking officers thought that I had done a great job. Crime had been reduced in the area, and I was left alone. But where did that leave me and my aspirations? How was I going to hit the big time and be 'Pinchy of the Flying Squad'?

I'd made many, many good friends in the police; they were like an extended family. It was as though I had lots of brothers who were there for me, backing me up, and me backing them up. It was so good to know that I was never alone in a work environment, and that I had continual support. We would cover each other all the way – from the arrest of a drunk to giving evidence at the Old Bailey. Outside of work, I socialised with many of my colleagues.

But things had changed. Unlike when I first joined, when we were given the 'nod' on how to be good coppers, with a heavy dose of compromise as long as the job got done, we had to be more cautious because of a 'softly softly' policing approach. We were always looking over our shoulders for fear of getting our knuckles rapped over any little misdemeanour. Practices that had once been commonplace were now taboo. The threat of imprisonment hung in the air as more policemen were getting arrested, and the high-ranking officers were totally unsupportive. I had gone from the dizzy heights of being one of the 'Top Dogs' to the dismal lows of being a copper that other people had to be wary of, in case I landed them in a lot of trouble. My breed of copper was fast becoming extinct in a jungle of political correctness.

My yearly appraisal had me facing the superintendent.

'Pinchbeck! Good to hear you've calmed down and taken a back seat.' He looked me in the eye and continued, 'You were on the slippery slope that leads to "gripping the rail" and I wouldn't want that to happen to you.'

'No, sir.' I knew he meant that if I carried on my heavy-handedness, I would end up in court facing a long prison sentence.

That very same evening Arsenal was playing Newcastle at home. I was on duty, going through the motions, very aware that I had to keep myself in check. At the end of the match there was a stand-off, tensions were running high and a battle between the two sets of supporters was in the air. A Newcastle supporter ran towards the Arsenal fans with his fist raised. Instinctively, I stepped in and decked him. Turning, I caught the eye of the superintendent, who shook his head.

'Leopards never change their spots,' he said.

Sheepishly, I ducked back into the police cordon, hiding myself from his scrutiny.

I had the council estates much under my control. My presence had a stabilising effect on the residents, which made my job a lot easier. Whenever I turned up, people would react to me in such a way that my ego was boosted, and that was a good feeling.

My heart at the time was like a block of granite, unbreakable, hard, uncaring. The only thing that affected me was – me. I was totally absorbed with myself. I was like an actor. Whenever I put on my uniform, it was as though I took on another persona. I was Mr Macho. It helped that physically I was heads taller than most people, and my build was such that no one really argued with me. But problems arose when this 'macho' Simon crept into my 'real' life. Then it became impossible to know the difference. Was I Simon the policeman, or Simon the husband and friend? It was like I was wearing a mask, one that I wore from the time I got up to the time I went to bed.

I wore the mask with my wife. At the time I didn't even think to ask her how she was, or if things were all right with her. I just assumed that she was OK; after all, she was married to me, we had a good home, we both worked, so we had money coming in. We never really argued, except for the times when I never phoned because I was out having a good time drinking – when I should have been at home with her. Whenever we went out to parties or dinner-dances, I would leave her with the women and I would spend the whole time with my buddies, drinking the bar dry. It was a sore point between us.

But, still the mask was in place – it became a permanent fixture. In truth, I didn't know who I really was. I performed for whoever was my audience. But inside, the huge void had never gone; it was still there. Inwardly, I was running on empty.

Then, early in 1984, Lynda announced that she was pregnant. I was overjoyed. Perhaps becoming a father would give me a real *purpose*, cause me to become more *me*!

My grandmother was a Catholic, and so was my mum. I was raised a Catholic but never followed the faith. The 'Hail Mary' and 'Our Father' had no effect on me. My gran was strong in her faith and went to Mass, and would encourage me to do the same. But I somehow knew that the answer to my life lay elsewhere.

Lynda and I regularly visited my parents in Burton-on-Trent. My sister, Ann Marie, was severely physically and mentally impaired, and her condition was such that many people found it difficult to relate to her, but Lynda, with her sweet, understanding nature, developed a rapport with her. One time, we were visiting whilst my sister was in respite care. We spent the days with my parents, taking them out; it was a nice break for them. But then my mum received a phone call and my parents rushed off to see my sister. Just over a week later, when Lynda and I were back in London, my mum phoned to say that my sister had died.

It was a terrible shock to me. Ann Marie was my one and only sister and, to make matters worse, the circumstances leading to her death were suspicious. But after investigations, the Coroner concluded that her death was a misadventure. Still, I couldn't believe it; one minute my sister was living with my parents, and the next, we were scattering her ashes. Was this all there was to life? Should I really be expecting something more?

I didn't tell a soul outside of the family that my sister had passed away – I kept it deep within, it was too painful to bring to the surface. But it wasn't long after her death that during a day shift I found myself walking into a church. I was surrounded by statues and candles. Somewhere deep inside I was hoping to experience *something* that would fill the emptiness, but although it was quiet and peaceful, I felt nothing. I walked out the same as I'd gone in, searching for . . . what? I didn't even know.

My son was born in September. Watching the birth, I was somewhat detached from Lynda's pain. When my son, Thomas, was laid in my arms, I was proud to be a dad and glad that I now had a legitimate reason to have a drink with the lads. And I did!

Drink was still playing a very big part in my life. I drank on duty, off duty, any time. On my beat was an

Irish guy who invited me into his home and gave me large amounts of his home brew, called poteen. It was made from potatoes and tasted awful, but it had a powerful punch. I'd stagger out of his house, drive the police car back to the station, and then drive my own car home. It never entered my head that what I was doing was morally wrong, and that I had arrested many people who drove under the influence. I drank more and more, and was still able to go to work and function; how, I don't know, but I did.

After ten years, I was offered the chance to move stations. I took it. I loved Holloway but I knew that it was time to move on. Many of my friends had either gone or were thinking of moving on, too.

My wife was pregnant again and the house we were living in was now too small. So a move to a bigger house in a new area was the right thing. Loughton in Essex was where our new police house was situated. I never knew such a place existed! Although it was a bit out in the sticks, both Lynda and I thought it would be a good place to raise our family. The station that I would be attached to was Barkingside, which was completely different to Holloway. In this area, people were more helpful towards the police.

At Barkingside, I began boxing again for the police and started playing rugby for a local club. My face was splattered across the pages of the local paper for either boxing or rugby, enhancing my fearless reputation once again.

Loughton at that time was an affluent area. Many 'respectable' criminals lived there and the surrounding places and I was involved with various crime squads. On many occasions, as part of my job, I had to enter criminal's houses as part of an investigation. It never

Simon boxing – Metropolitan Police v RAF.

Simon with Tom and Jamie.

Simon on his 50th birthday with Jamie, Lynda and Tom.

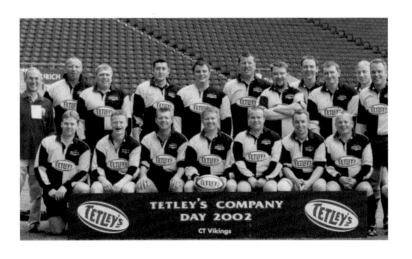

Twickenham 2002 – Simon back row, first left.

Tough Talk street outreach in Ayr, Scotland.

The Tough Talk team at a street outreach in Ilford.

Martyn, Adam, Ian, Joe and Simon.

Arthur demonstrating the deadlift.

ceased to amaze me how some people profited so richly from crime. The houses were huge, with expensive ornaments, flash cars in the drive . . . This was the life I wanted.

On the beat one hot afternoon, a large, shiny, new Audi saloon coasted alongside me. The window smoothly went down and a loud cockney voice said, "'Ere, Walrus! Fancy seeing you 'ere!'

Peering into the car I was shocked to see one of the old Arsenal boys.

'You've done all right for yourself, I see,' I remarked.

He grinned. 'You know how it is. A bit of this, a bit of that. That's life, ain't it!'

As he drove off, I stared after him. Here I was, busting a gut trying to keep law and order, when those breaking the law were living a better life than me.

'It's time my life changed,' I muttered. 'And for the better!'

5

Towards the Rocks

I had a lovely wife and two terrific boys, a new car, a bigger house, and I was working close to home. There should have been no stress of any kind yet *still* there was a hole in my life. My children were going to a Catholic school and, at times, they would come home with pictures of Jesus and tell me about things they had learnt about the Bible. None of it touched me. One of the main reasons I was happy they'd got into such a school was that I knew my gran would be pleased, and that meant a lot to me. But I felt I was still searching for that elusive 'something' – what was it? I didn't know. I would look around and see my friends and colleagues all happy and content. And then there was me. What was wrong with me? I couldn't work it out.

All my big ideas about getting into the CID and living real live episodes of *The Sweeney* had been shot to pieces. I had purposely taken another route in my career and had opted to be back in uniform. The quiet life out in the sticks in Buckhurst Hill had been all right for a while, but I was finding it increasingly dull. I wanted *action*; I wanted to be back on top again.

A lifeline came my way when I saw an advertisement in the *Police Gazette* about recruiting for the Territorial

Support Group, based in Paddington, west London. I jumped at the chance to break away from the backwoods of Buckhurst Hill and hit the 'action button' of the West End.

Entrance into the TSG was in two parts. I flew through the fitness test, no problem. The second part was an interview. At first, the superintendent was asking me straightforward questions – 'So rugby is your favourite pastime, you say? Hmm. Your record of arrests is quite impressive, isn't it?' – at this stage I thought I was well on my way to joining up. Then he said, 'What about your complaints record?' His eyes bore into mine. Taking a deep breath, I responded, 'I will admit I've had a few.'

'A few!' He leaned down beside his chair and when he came up again, he had a stack of paper. He slammed it down. The pile slithered across the desk and he said, 'How do you account for all these?'

'That was at Holloway. I'm a changed man now. I'm married with children. That life is behind me now,' I said. I knew I was battling for my career.

Anyway, he relented and I successfully enrolled into the TSG. And the next five years were the best time of my police career.

I was physically fit. As part of the TSG you were expected to work out every day, and I did. I trained in firearms, surveillance, and enhanced my driving skills. The TSG was the cutting edge of policing. The incidents that we had to deal with were really juicy – action-packed – and I was able to use my new skills to the uttermost. Every day was different.

It was a cold March morning when our unit was called to a flat on a council estate in west London. Apparently, a man had gone mad and was waving an axe about. Then he'd gone into his flat, barricaded the door, and wouldn't open up. All efforts to talk him out failed. I smashed the door down and charged inside, with my colleagues close behind me holding up their shields. The man, with manic eyes, ran out of one of the rooms waving the axe above his head. He brought the axe down, and one of my colleagues deflected the blow with his shield. As they forced him to the ground, I wrenched the axe out of his hand, threw it to safety, then quickly hand-cuffed him. It was a job to get him into the police van, but his neighbours were outside cheering us on.

That evening in the pub, it was like old times for me, just like when I was in Holloway, only better. I was sur-rounded by friends who had become, once again, like an extended family. We shared the same thoughts and atti-tudes. The younger policemen had never heard of me, but liked the way I carried myself, so they sort of looked up to me. It did my ego good.

The social side of the TSG was party-time most nights. I could drink anyone under the table. Once again, I rele-gated my wife and kids to the back burner. I provided food and clothing and my presence – sometimes. I didn't stop to think about what effect my long absences were having on my family. Lynda never shouted or demanded things from me so I just assumed she was fine with the way we were living. My selfishness was all-consuming; I never once gave a thought to how anyone, let alone my wife, was feeling. To be honest, I didn't care.

Football loomed up again whilst I was part of the TSG. My unit regularly assisted the Central London Football Intelligence Unit which worked from Scotland Yard. The CLFIU obtained information concerning games where organised violence was going to occur. We became very familiar with the 'known faces' of soccer trouble. I was in my element, reliving the days of glory when I was at Highbury. The Walrus was reborn!

One violent incident happened when Arsenal was playing at the Millwall ground, 'The Den'. My unit met up with the Arsenal fans at a pub in Mile End Road. The atmosphere was charged with tension, but we escorted the fans safely to The Den. Following the match, we knew the Arsenal fans had gone back to the pub but we didn't know where the Millwall supporters were. Then one of my colleagues got a call to inform us that the Millwall fans were coming into Stepney Green station – not far from the pub. Jumping out of the police van, we ran up the road to the Underground station entrance to confront the Millwall fans, in the hope that we could contain them. But it was too late. To our right, the Millwall supporters were stomping towards us. To our left, tanked up with alcohol and drugs, were the Arsenal fans. We were stuck in the middle. Flashbacks of the time I was caught up between the Arsenal and West Ham fans sprang into my mind. My heart raced as flares shot into the air, bricks were thrown and bottles smashed on the pavement. Both sets of fans were shouting and swearing, eager to get to each other. My unit was like a very thin line that separated the two groups. We were not successful. The men on both sides launched into one another. I began to beat off the arms and legs that were attacking me, with my baton. Fear reared up inside me; my uniform was wet with sweat. I knew that if I fell to the ground I would be dead. Through sheer panic I battled with all my might to keep the opposing forces apart.

Reinforcements came as more policemen got involved in trying to keep the peace. The battle raged for a couple of hours, the side streets were peppered with opposing fans attacking one another, but the smaller numbers were easier to contain and I was able to regain my confidence.

Later, as I propped up the bar in the local pub in
Paddington, my colleagues praised me: 'Did you see
Pinchy? What a nutter!', 'Did you see him hit that bloke
with his baton? He was lethal' and 'Glad Punchy-Pinchy
was there to back us up'. I could have drowned in a sea
of pride. Yet, I knew deep down that something wasn't
quite right. I wish now that I had spoken to someone,
and told them what I was really feeling inside – that
when my anger reared up, it caused me to reach a peak
that made me lose all sense of time and place; I just
wanted to lash out, crush and trample on anything in
my way, and this *frightened* me. What was it that made
me behave in that way? It was scary knowing that I
could easily lose total control and that I might injure
someone fatally. But if I had disclosed my real identity, I
would have probably been ordered to go off sick and see
a psychiatrist.

During this period, the yearning for money had buried
itself . . . until I went to Florida.

A friend of Lynda had just come back from Orlando
and had raved about how wonderful it was. So, Lynda
and I decided to take the kids and, boy, it lived up to my
expectations.

The car that I hired was one of the biggest, with air
conditioning, electric windows, plush seats; it was luxury to the max! The hotels that we stayed in were world
class. For me, it was like living the film-star life. The
food was great, the weather agreeable, the people
friendly. I felt at home.

I had taken out a loan for the family holiday and I
knew it would take me two years to pay it off. Two *years*!
Many English people on the flight home were talking
about one thing: 'How can we leave England and settle
in Florida?' I got caught up in the various conversations

but, for me, it wasn't just talk. I really, truly wanted to leave my old life behind and go to the States. Maybe this was the answer I'd been looking for. Perhaps this was the thing that was going to fill the void, bringing peace of mind, making me feel whole. But one thing I knew for sure – I could not do this on a policeman's wages. There had to be another way for me to earn the type of cash I needed. On the flight home, I was obsessed – how could I get this sort of money? Would promotion bring it in? Maybe moonlighting? Or was there another way?

I had been in the Territorial Support Group for nearly five years. I had a choice of renewing my contract for another five years, or leaving for fresh pastures. The TSG had been a great time in my life, I had made some great friends, but I felt that perhaps it might be the right time for me to go.

One of my work colleagues was involved in an accident which really affected me. He was riding his motorbike late one night and was in a serious collision in which he lost his leg. I was at work that night, and when the call came in I was devastated. He was such a nice guy. Whenever there was a meeting, or a gathering that was boring, quiet or mundane, when he showed up everything changed; he was such a bright spark. I visited him in hospital, and he still managed to be cheerful and focused. But I found it hard to come to terms with what had happened to him. Why did this have to happen to such a good guy? Why did criminals and evil people seem to escape bad things happening to them? What did my mate do to deserve this? The questions would roll around my mind, tormenting me.

My only problem with leaving the TSG was, what was I going to do? I wanted to make money and lots of it, but the difficulty was – how? Then I got a phone call from another mate of mine. He called me out of the blue for a chat, and I mentioned that I was leaving the TSG.

'Why don't you come to Enfield?' he said. 'We could do with a bloke like you.'

'Enfield? I don't know.'

He really sold the idea to me, and within a few months I was based at Enfield, in uniform, patrolling the streets. But, before I left the TSG, I wanted to do something *different* with the many friends I had made. My mate who had lost his leg had been discharged from hospital, and had got himself engaged. So we decided to have a joint 'do' – his stag night and my leaving. We went to Amsterdam.

The red-light district was fascinating. I had never seen anything like it before – women being paraded in shop windows for men to ogle them. The live sex shows were unbelievable and I knew that I would never see such things at home. The Amsterdam trip truly 'broadened my mind'.

By the time we got back to England, I had decided to change my car. I bought a brand new Mercedes. I was able to pay for it by borrowing money. Yet, I wasn't satisfied. Driving my car would bring envious stares but there was a deep yearning within me that I was still unable to quench. If anyone had asked me what I wanted most, a truthful answer would have been, 'I don't know.' I didn't know what I was really looking for. And every time I did get whatever it was I *thought* I wanted, the desire for that 'thing' I was missing grew stronger. Consequently, I was restless, dissatisfied, confused and unhappy. But no way was I going to share my thoughts with anyone.

Enfield was a lot different from the TSG. It was more mundane and every day was nearly the same. The people

I worked with in Enfield were just not on my wavelength. I wanted to punch people into submission and they wanted to 'talk' – what a clash of interests!

Around this time, my eldest son was leaving his junior school, and I was adamant that I wanted him to go to a Christian secondary school. This wasn't because either Lynda or I had any affection for God. Most people I knew wanted their children to go to a Christian school for the simple fact that the standard of education was better. So, Lynda and I decided to attend church. I'd look at the parishioners lighting candles, chanting the prayers off by heart, hanging onto every word that came out of the mouth of the priest. It was meaningless to me, and I thought the people were hypocrites. I stuck it out just so that I could get my son into a good school. I even started a youth club for the church, but there was no Bible study or anything to do with God; it was all about having a good time and keeping the young people off the streets. Anyway, my son Tom did go to our school of choice, so as far as I was concerned, it was all a worthwhile exercise.

After a while, an opportunity arose in the Enfield Task Unit and I jumped at the chance. The Task Unit was mainly undercover work, which meant that I was out of uniform and in plain clothes. Most of my work colleagues were young single men, who knew how to have a good time. I soon adopted the single-life mindset; I had an earlobe pierced and my left arm tattooed. Most nights I was out clubbing with my new-found friends. My wife and sons hardly ever saw me and, when I was at home, I had a deep hunger to get up and go out. Mixing with young people had me doing things that young people did. I began to experiment with recreational drugs which caused me to believe that I was 'living the life'. The distance between Lynda and I grew wider. She would ask, 'Simon, what have I done wrong?'

and I would ignore her because I knew that she hadn't done a thing wrong. *I* knew what was wrong, but at that time I wasn't prepared to put it right. The truth was I didn't *want* to put it right. I didn't care.

My mother-in-law was very ill for a while and Lynda was beside herself with worry, but it just didn't bother me. I was out until the early hours of the morning enjoying myself. Lynda needed me, but I wasn't there for her. She even arranged a surprise fortieth birthday party for me. It was a great party – lots of my friends and family were there – yet I never even thanked her.

Lynda's mum was diagnosed as being terminally ill. My wife divided her time between the hospital and looking after our sons, whilst holding down a full-time job. She lost weight, and looked weary and burdened. Whenever I was at home, she would either have come back from the hospital or was just about to leave with our two sons in tow. I would breeze into the house, happy in the knowledge that my dinner was cooked and I had a clean shirt to wear for my night out with the lads.

I began to resent the hurt looks from my wife and the unhappy glances from my sons whenever I was getting ready to go out.

'Where are you going, Simon? I really need you here.'

'I don't want to be here, and it's none of your business where I'm going, so don't ask me.' I would slam the door, or stomp up the stairs.

As Lynda's mum's condition grew steadily worse, I knew my wife was battling hard to hold herself, and the boys, together. She needed me to support her emotionally, physically and mentally. My sons needed their father, as their mother was under a lot of pressure. But I was not concerned about my wife or her mother.

I left, not for one minute aware that I was steering the ship of my life towards jagged rocks.

6

Hero to Zero

I was filled with excitement at the thought of having a place of my own. I could have parties every night, all night if I wanted to. I could eat junk food, I could get bombed out of my mind. It didn't matter; there would be no one around to frown upon my behaviour, or to ask me pointless, annoying questions. Pulling out of the drive-way, Lynda happened to be driving in. Our eyes locked. Her haunting, pleading stare did not penetrate my hard heart. I dismissed it as I drove off to my new life.

A friend of mine was going on a round-the-world trip and I'd offered to look after his house while he was gone. So it was easy for me to leave, as I had a place to stay for a few months until I could sort out what I really wanted to do with my life.

My house – a wonderful, spacious place – was like a beacon of light to the young guys I worked with. Many were either living in bed-sits or at home with their parents. None had a whole house to themselves. So, I was never alone. When the clubs and pubs were shut, every-one was welcome back at Pinchy's.

Looking at my bank balance made me feel a bit depressed. I was living in a fantastic house, a Mercedes parked out front – and I was broke! I took the car back to the dealer and bought a Vauxhall. My wages were tied up before I even earned them; I was now running two households and it was financially crippling. I needed more money, and fast. So I went to see my bank manager and arranged for a £10,000 increase on the mortgage of my home. Lynda was none the wiser. At last, I felt as though I had 'arrived'. I was in my own home, sitting on a little nest egg that I could spend any way I chose. My wife and boys were OK, as far as I could see – now was the time for me to live!

I would go and see Lynda and the boys just to touch base with family life. Lynda would ask, 'How are you, Simon?' and I'd say, 'Fine, love, just trying to get my head together, you know,' as I tucked into a lovely meal that she had cooked especially for me. I would spend time with the boys, watching TV, relaxing around my family. Sometimes I would spend the night with Lynda. I was so selfish; I was happy with my double life but I didn't see that breezing in and out of my family like this was upsetting them. Whenever I was at home, I was husband and Dad, then once I left, I would slip into my persona as a single man. Lynda would at times beg me to move back home, but I didn't. If she went on too much I would leave.

Work began to get in the way of my partying. Even though I loved my job my mind was never fully on it as I was always planning what I was going to do that evening. I loved the freedom of doing whatever I wanted to do, and the first few months of this new life flew by. Then, reality began to sink in. A mountain of washing was never dealt with, unless I did it. The washing-up piled up. Dust gathered and nobody was getting rid of it. Nights started to get lonely. When I closed the front door, the silence was deafening. I would lie in bed staring at the ceiling wondering, 'Is this really what I want?' The emptiness inside me was still there.

I decided to have a bit more contact with my sons so I collected them from Lynda and brought them back to my 'bachelor pad'. They walked in, tentatively, and sat on the edge of the settee. Whatever I offered them, they refused. I felt like a stranger to them. I could see I had gone from hero to zero in their eyes and yet I didn't want to go home; I wanted to squeeze everything I could out of this exciting new life.

Still the emptiness persisted and I began to realise that somewhere along the line, I had lost the plot. My mind was mashed up and it was hard to focus on a single, rational thought. Anger and aggression were never far away from me. The dissatisfaction of my life invariably spilled over into my work. My colleagues found it hard to talk to me, as I would snap their heads off. Criminals who showed any sign of lying or 'attitude' ended up on the receiving end of my very bad temper. I was spiralling out of control.

Then I got talking to a few friends and someone mentioned seeing a clairvoyant. I thought, 'This could be the answer,' so I made an appointment. I was really excited, especially when the clairvoyant told me I was going to be a big success and come into a lot of money. This was *exactly* what I wanted to hear. I floated out of her house. I wanted a huge pot of money, a big house and all the trappings. I wanted to swan around like a multimillionaire. The idea of living in Florida along Millionaire's Row seemed like it could become a reality.

From that first meeting, I couldn't get enough of clairvoyants. I became addicted to seeing anyone who could predict my future, especially if it was good stuff! I saw an astrologer, read my horoscopes, visited New Age shops and bought self-help books that I thought would enhance my life. I became totally consumed with seeking help and advice from this occult source. I wore crystal necklaces and kept crystals in my pocket. I bought miniature Buddhas to keep in the house as the concept of Buddhism was interesting to me. I thought I was 'a good bloke' and therefore, according to Buddhists, whatever good I did would come back to me. Well, in that case, I thought, I was definitely due for a big pay out!

Christmas 1997 saw me getting dressed in my expensive gear on Christmas Eve, raring to go out with my friends. We were planning to spend the night at a nightclub in north London where I had done a lot of undercover work. As I sprayed on my aftershave, I thought fleetingly of past Christmas Eves; wrapping presents and filling stockings with Lynda, the smiling, happy faces of Tom and Jamie . . . Quickly brushing those thoughts away, I jumped into my car and drove off.

Christmas and Boxing Day were spent with my family. I enjoyed the food and the company. Visiting my parents was really just continuing the 'Happy Family' image – which was a lie. Then, in January, Lynda's mum died. All the time my mother-in-law was ill and I wasn't at home, she never judged me, but continued to accept me right up until she drew her last breath. I made myself available to Lynda in helping with the funeral arrangements. At the cemetery, Lynda held herself together, but I could tell that she was devastated. I could see she was thinking, 'I'm alone, no mother, no husband.' I'd found the single life wasn't all it was cracked up to be, and right then, I wanted to be back in the fold of my family; I wanted the love of my wife and boys. Also, my friend whose house I was staying in was coming back from his trip. It seemed like a good excuse to go home now.

I moved back home and quickly settled in. I wanted to pick up from where I had left off six months before. But I had not reckoned on the emotional and mental state of my wife and kids. Whenever I was in the same room as my boys, the air was icy. There was absolutely no warmth in their voices. If I told them to do something, especially my youngest son, the answer would be, 'Why do you want me to do that? Why don't you clear off and leave us alone?'

It was really painful. Lynda was wired up and couldn't seem to relax.

'Where're you going?' she would ask, every time I went out.

I was getting more and more confused, frustrated and angry. What was the point of life? Nothing I did seemed to ease the discontent and unhappiness. Tensions would cause pressure to block my thoughts and I had flashbacks of when I was attacked by football fans – this would bring on panic attacks. I decided to see my doctor, and told him about my anger and flashbacks. He put me on a course of antidepressants, and I also had an appointment to see a psychiatrist.

'You're suffering from post-traumatic stress disorder,' he told me.

I felt relieved to give it a name, but he never gave me any clear advice on how I could get rid of it. Also, I now had the added burden of keeping my visits to the psychiatrist a secret. At work, occupational therapy treatment was available, but I knew that that would be like sounding the death knell for a macho guy like me. On patrol, I would go berserk for no reason. Football fans would be drunkenly singing in the street and I would lash out at them, punching and knocking them about. I knew it was wrong, but it was as though I couldn't help myself. My mind was in orbit and when I went crazy, I was somehow able to deal with it. I was fortunate that my uniform was able to protect me from violent retaliation. My colleagues just took my irrational outbursts as part of the persona of 'Pinchy' so I knew I could get away with it. No one had an inkling of the pressure that was building up inside of me.

I had tried everything: single life, married life, drinking, partying, fighting, fortune-tellers, New Age philosophy, psychiatry, religion – nothing was working for me. Who or what had the answer?

The bills were still coming in, my wages were going out. Lynda's mum had left her some money. I persuaded her to buy a BMW and we booked a family holiday in Lanzarote which left us with just a small amount of money. But our relationship was going nowhere; Lynda was trying hard to get us both back on track, but to be truthful, I was a lost cause. I was totally selfish.

I was attending the police gym every day, five days a week. Then, I got a cheap deal for membership at a sports club in Chigwell. It was the business. The police gym had just basic training equipment, but this club was far, far above it in terms of facilities. It was plush, modern, and you met up with a different class of person. Making friends was no problem. I got chatting with some guys who were local 'faces' and they knew of me, which wasn't surprising given their nature of work. These guys quickly became friends with me and I began to train regularly with them. Afterwards, we would have a chat. Our friendship grew and we began to meet up outside of the gym.

I knew they were villains, but it didn't make me, as a policeman, want to dissociate myself from them. Rather, their notoriety made me want to hang out with them all the more. They had bundles of cash, flash cars, nice clothes, pretty girls and they had a confidence about them. I was very happy to have made their acquaintance. I would be introduced to their friends as, 'This is Simon, he's one of us,' which would bring a smile to my face. However, I noticed that whenever they received certain phone calls, they would glance at me and then walk to the other side of the room.

A guy called Benny and I became good mates, so when he suggested that I should take up boxing training as well, I was up for it. I met him at a pub in High Beach for a bout of sparring. It was a 'known' club and, as Benny introduced his brother Clive to me, I instantly recognised his face from football intelligence – Clive was an ardent West Ham supporter.

My reputation as a boxer circulated in the club and people respected me as someone who could handle himself. Here I was, once again, getting attention through my aggressive, forceful nature. One afternoon one of the local 'hard men' who had heard about me decided to challenge me to a bit of sparring. He was a big guy, like me. I heard him call out, 'Let me in with the copper, I'll sort him out,' and he clambered into the ring, and stood facing me. One look at his face told me he wanted to do me damage. I was definitely up for it. A surge of anger and strength overtook me and by the second round they had to carry him out.

Moving with these guys opened up a whole new world for me. They had an endless supply of money and they were fun to be with. My lifestyle changed; instead of going out with my police friends, I would now go out with criminals. My new friends were constantly calling me – 'Si, doing anything? I'll pick you up in an hour, we'll have something to eat', 'Si, I'm going up the club, do you want a lift?' My wife was at the end of her tether. 'Are you going out again, Simon? You were out last night, and the night before . . .' But her words were lost on me. I would mumble something and I was out of the door. I was becoming engulfed in the criminal fraternity without fully realising it.

One day, Benny told me, 'I'm thinking of taking a course of the gear. What do you reckon?'

I knew he meant steroids. I had never taken them before, and never would have. But, because Benny was planning to take some, I said, 'Count me in,' and within a matter of days I was injecting myself with steroids. The ampoules were written in Spanish and it never dawned on me that I could be injecting myself with anything – I could've died. But the powerful pull of my friendship with Benny and the other guys was so strong, I was happy to participate in whatever they were into, whenever they decided to include me.

Taking the steroids made me train even harder. I pushed and pushed myself for no reason other than I wanted to look good. My trips to the clairvoyant increased, too; she was telling me my future looked rosy. This was what I wanted to hear. Yet my mind was getting more and more confused. When I was at work, I was one of the lads, eager to catch wrongdoers and put them away. Then, I would mix with the very criminals that I should be putting away, having a great time! I was a mess, heading for a fall, and I didn't even know it.

The inspector of my Task Unit was retiring and, as usual in the police, a 'do' was being held for him. The night started off in the pub with a couple of drinks, then we all went on to a nightclub. The music was swinging, the drinks were flowing. My body was in peak condition and I knew I was looking good. On the dance floor I was having a laugh but slowly, for no real reason, I began to get a bit agitated. As people nudged me or walked past me I started to get a bit paranoid, lashing out with my elbows and shoulders. I wasn't sure what was happening to me, but I began not to feel like myself. I felt hot and troubled and the noise and voices seemed to make me worse.

It was about 2.30 in the morning and the group I was with told me that they were leaving.

'I'll catch up with you in a sec, I've just got to say a few goodbyes,' I said. Leaving the bar area, I walked towards the dance area – some of the people I wanted to speak with were dancing. As my foot touched the dance floor, the flashing lights, the loud music and the smoke overtook me. I became disorientated, confused. I heard shouting and screaming. Faces loomed at me, but they were not the faces of the clubbers. I was caught up between Arsenal and West Ham soccer thugs. The faces were contorted as they hurled angry abuse at me. These were the same faces that had been tormenting me on and off for a while. Fear gripped me and my heartbeat increased.

'They're going to kill me!' I thought. Panic welled up inside me. 'It's either them or me.' I shouted, 'Noooooooo!' All the aggression and tension inside me just burst. I lashed out with my fists. Then I blacked out.

Stumbling into a cab office with blood pouring from the back of my right hand, I knew that I had been in some kind of fight, but I had no idea about the details.

'A and E, mate,' I told the controller.

All the way to the hospital I kept shaking my head to try and clear my mind so that I could remember what had happened. But I couldn't.

At the hospital, they cleaned the wound and said I needed a few stitches. I told the doctor I had fallen over and hurt my hand – which they believed. But when

Lynda came to pick me up, and I told her the same story, she did not seem to believe me at all.

After a few hours of sleep, I was up and ready for work. I was having a bit of breakfast when the doorbell rang. Opening the door I was a bit surprised to see one of my colleagues standing on the doorstep.

'Come in, mate,' I said.

He remained outside. 'Pinchy, you've really done it now. You've hit the wrong bloke.'

'What you talking about?'

'At the club last night . . . you hit Jack good and square in the mouth, knocked his teeth out.'

I couldn't take in what he was saying, because I just could not remember what I had done the night before.

'Pinchy, listen to me. They're after you now. You've just gone too far and they're going to throw the book at you.'

I looked at the bandages wrapped around my hand. My mind jumped and weaved about. 'What have I done? There's bound to be witnesses.' I thought of all the near misses that I had had whilst in the force. Time after time I had got away with things – would I escape again?

7

When One Door Shuts . . .

My heart was pounding as I climbed into an unmarked police car. My mind was in a whirl; I couldn't believe that this was happening to me. Perhaps I did punch the guy to the floor and knock his teeth out, but to drag me, officially, to see the super was taking things too far! Still, it was probably just a formality. Wasn't it?

'Pinchbeck, there is an allegation that you were involved in a serious assault on a fellow police officer at a nightclub in the early hours of this morning. There is going to be an investigation. I'm suspending you from duty on full pay. Please hand me your warrant card.'

My mouth was dry. For the past twenty years this warrant card had never left my possession. Reluctantly I gave my card to the superintendent.

'Collect your belongings and you'll be escorted off the premises.'

Sitting in my car outside my house I wondered how Lynda was going to take my news. I thought, after everything I'd put her through, this would be the final straw.

'What do you mean you've been suspended? You told me that you fell over. How did you go from falling over to punching some guy's teeth out of his head? Simon, how can you do this to me?'

'Listen, love. This'll all be over soon and, before you know it, I'll be back out working, getting extra money from my overtime and our lives will be back on track.'

In struck me that ten, fifteen years ago, if I'd knocked another officer out, I would probably have been told to pay his dentistry bill and that would have been that. But not now.

I'd thought that maybe being suspended was a good opportunity for me to have a break, clear my head. But instead of enjoying my first few days of freedom from work, I was hospitalised. The punch had damaged my hand so badly that it swelled up to twice its normal size and I developed septicaemia. Then, when I'd recovered, Lynda drove me home from hospital, and we had a blazing row.

'Your mate from work told me you're going to get about eighteen months. What am I supposed to do while you're banged up?'

'No, love, no. He's talking rubbish. This is going to blow over soon and I'll be back on duty. I've got some good people on the case. Please, love, trust me in this situation. I'm going to make everything better. You'll see. Don't worry, and don't listen to anyone who tells you otherwise.' As the words were coming out of my mouth, I didn't have a clue how in the world I would be able to right this situation. It was true; I *could* be looking at eighteen months, banged up with some hard cons.

During the first few weeks of my suspension, I was secretly hoping for a phone call that would wipe away all my worries and fears about the case. Instead, I got a call from Edmonton Police Station headquarters to inform me that I had to attend a formal interview about the allegations.

'The charge is one of Assault, Occasioning Actual Bodily Harm.' The detective chief inspector handed me my charge sheet with a court date for three weeks' time. I was taken to the fingerprinting and photographing room, a place I had taken other people millions of times. I could not believe this was happening to me.

'It's going to blow over, you wait and see,' I said to Lynda. 'Once my psychiatric report is read, the case will be dropped and I'll walk away from all of this.' But the expression on her face told me that she did not believe what I was saying.

A few weeks and a couple of court appearances later, I had to face the fact that this situation was not going to simply go away. I would have to take on the might of the Criminal Justice System. I knew that coppers who have done wrong are very much frowned upon in society, and a policeman doing time is a hated convict. Life in prison for me would be a nightmare, dangerous from beginning to end. I had to clear my name!

The case was at committal stage and my options were to be tried in front of a judge and jury which would happen at a Crown Court; or face a magistrate and have my fate decided by one or three people. From my police experience I knew that I would stand a better chance of getting a 'not guilty' in front of a jury. My case was committed to Crown Court and I knew I had a long wait before I made my appearance.

Money was becoming an issue. I needed more money coming in. Then I met a friend of mine at the sports club and he advised me to borrow money against my endowment policy. I never knew you could do that but I found out that he was right and £12,000 was given to me within days of my telephone call to the insurance company. I could've had up to £26,000 but I stopped at twelve as I thought that that would be enough for my needs. The drawback was that I would have to pay £70 per month interest, but I wasn't worried about paying anything back just yet. What a fool I had become!

Once the money was deposited into my account, I took my family on holiday to Germany partly because Lynda's mum was German and I thought it might be good for her to see where her mum came from. It was a nice break, fresh country air and beautiful scenery.

Back home, my police friends had all but disappeared from my life. No one contacted me. I was on my own. My trips to the sports club proved fruitful though because I acquired a lot of new friends who seemed more in tune with me than my ex-colleagues. My 'new' family would often take me out for meals. Our training times helped us to bond. One of them, a professional boxer called Laurie, became a close friend. He often came to my house, and we trained regularly at the club. He introduced me to a lot of his friends. They knew I was a copper, yet they all accepted me.

Laurie knew about my case being committed to court and asked me what I was doing for money.

'Not a lot, really. Why, have you got something for me?'

'Well, it's not much, but I wouldn't mind if you came along with me when I collected some debts. What do you reckon?'

I shrugged. I didn't want to get into any kind of trouble, but I needed the money. So I found myself doing a few jobs for Laurie, getting back money that was owed.

Throughout the year I was waiting for my court date, I tried to get as much money as I could for Lynda and the boys in case things went pear-shaped. But I told Lynda, 'Even if I do get found guilty, there is no way that they will put me in prison. I may get a fine or even community service, but prison – no way.' How I hoped my words would come true!

Lynda was suffering, again because of me. My sons were suffering too. Their school work and behaviour was messed up so much that I was called in to see their heads of year. I explained the pressure my boys were under, which in turn explained why they were behaving irrationally.

Eventually, I found myself standing in the dock, swearing on the Bible that I would tell the truth. It was like being in a nightmare. The evidence for the prosecution appeared to be very strong. If the case had finished at that point, I would certainly have gone to prison. But once my defence started, the case began to slowly turn around. I had some very good character references from people in the police force but it was the psychiatric report which really swung the pendulum in my favour. The fact that I had been to see the doctor and the psychiatrist before the assault was the most salient point in the case. But was the jury going to believe that in my mind I was actually fighting off football hooligans that were threatening my life, or would they believe that I really wanted to punch the guy off the face of the earth? The waiting was torture.

The five days had taken its toll on me. I had lost my appetite and could not sleep. I spent hours going through every single aspect of the case – the comment of the judge; the evidence of the witnesses; my testimony . . . Had enough been done to ensure that I would get a 'not guilty' verdict, or had there been loose ends that would bring about my conviction?

Standing in the dock with two prison officers on either side of me, I watched the jury file in. The last juror, a lady, looked at me and smiled. I didn't know if that was good or bad. Then the jury foreman stood up. The judge asked him, 'Have you reached a verdict?'

'Yes, Your Honour.'

'How do you find the defendant, guilty or not guilty?'
'Not guilty.'

I shouted out 'Yes!', clenching my fists in a boxer's stance.

It was over, finished. I had got off, but the door was closing on my police career. What did life have in store for me now?

'Congratulations on getting a not guilty verdict, Simon. What plans do you have for your future?'

I shifted the phone to my other ear and said, 'I'm thinking of taking a medical discharge.'

A deep sigh was followed by the chief superintendent's relieved voice. 'That's exactly what we thought. I'll get the wheels in motion and we'll do this sooner rather than later.'

Well, I thought, it had worked out quite nicely; I'd got off the charge and now I was honourably leaving the police force with a tidy pension to help me in my old age . . .

I was called to Headquarters to sign my discharge papers. A young boy, a fresh-faced school-leaver, met with me and led me to an office. He seated me at a small desk and handed me some papers.

'Could you sign at the Xs, please.'

'Hold on a minute, mate,' I said. 'I've done over twenty years in the service. Is no one of any rank going to come and say "Goodbye, have a nice life" or something?'

He looked at me a bit nervously and replied, 'No one's been booked to meet you but I . . .' He feebly held out his hand.

'Do yourself a favour,' I said, 'don't embarrass yourself.' I quickly signed the papers, and handed them back to him.

'Erm . . . what about your warrant card?'

For the second time, I had to give it up. Walking away from him, I called over my shoulder, 'I'll post it to you. All right?'

The lift door opened at the ground floor, and a huge weight of emptiness descended on me.

'Is this it?' I thought, bitterly. 'All the days, months, years I've devoted my life to being a policeman, and this is *it*?' Usually whenever a policeman was leaving the force for whatever reason a good drink-up was the order of the day. For me there was nothing. No retirement card. No present. No collection of money or vouchers. Zilch. I was angry and resentful. But then I felt a determination to succeed and this lifted my spirits a little.

It's been said that when one door shuts another one opens, and the door that opened for me was through Laurie, who put on a double celebration: for leaving the police force and for retiring and entering into a new phase of my life. It was held in a Chinese restaurant in Brentwood, Essex, and about twenty guys I'd got to know through Laurie attended. We must have ordered everything on the menu and the wine list, and it made me realise that feeling sorry for myself about how I had been treated by the police was wasting precious time. *This* was now my life and my one ambition was to make it a huge success, with all my dreams becoming reality.

Laurie became like a brother to me. We usually saw each other every day. We trained together and met up in the evenings. My relationship with him was like a lifeline. I hadn't got a job at this point and he would get me a bit of work, debt collecting. But Lynda was not happy about this.

'Simon, why don't you look for something stable, like a bit of security work? Or perhaps you could retrain . . .'

Shaking my head I told her no. And to appease her I booked up a holiday – where to? Where else but Florida! We had a great time and, when we came back, Laurie contacted me with offers of more work. I could sense a change, though; somehow the work had intensified and an element had been added that made me very uneasy – violence. I could handle myself and I didn't take any nonsense from anyone, but what was happening on each job we did now was unnerving me. One time, Laurie really went to town on the geezer, and I thought, we could be looking at five to ten years.

Benny was still on the scene, too. Once, we were in a coffee bar and he introduced me to his mate, Rod. Rod was broad-shouldered, good-looking and knew how to kit himself out. He had an eye for the ladies; he seemed a likeable rogue, not a threat or a danger to be around. In fact, he was quite entertaining.

I had told them both about the work I was doing with Laurie and how it was getting a bit out of hand.

'You're risking your liberty for a few quid? You're mad, mate,' said Rod.

Benny was nodding his head. 'I have to agree, Si, you're earning peanuts and if it went pear-shaped, you'd be going under. Get out while you're ahead.'

I knew they were right, but if I stopped working with Laurie, what would I do? I couldn't get a nine to five job and I didn't want to retrain. Earning regular money did not buy you a beautiful house in Florida, or cause you to experience life in the fast lane. I wanted to earn 'proper' money, but how?

By mutual agreement, I stopped working with Laurie. I liked him, but in truth, I was relieved our working partnership had ended. For the next few weeks I was hanging around the house, wondering what I could do to bring some more money in. Then, Rod called me out of the blue. We arranged to meet for a coffee and he soon had me laughing at his stories about some of the things he got up to. Then he hit me with a casual, 'Are you good on a radio?' He curved his hand as though he was holding a walkie-talkie.

'Should be! I've been using one for over twenty years.'

'OK. I've got a bit of work for you. I'll ring you tonight.' He looked at me for a second and slowly nodded his head. 'I'm going to take a chance on you, Si.'

'OK.' I felt good about this new development.

Later that night, Rod picked me up in his car and drove us somewhere outside of London. It was nearly midnight and I wasn't too sure where we were heading. Then he stopped the car, picked up two radios from the back seat, tuned them in and gave me one. Climbing out of the car, he said to me: 'Watch my back. I won't be long.'

Rod walked towards a large house and was gone. I sat in the car in the quiet street in the dark, hoping that he would come back soon. I wasn't sure what was going down, and I didn't feel that I could ask him. Within half an hour he was back, carrying a bag which he dumped in the boot. Soon we were out of the area, heading for home.

Pulling up in the street where I had parked my car, Rod turned to me and said, 'You've done well tonight.'

I stuffed the wad of notes he'd given me into my pocket and walked towards my car. 'Thanks, Rod, anytime.' The money he had given me was more than I had ever earned with Laurie – it was a couple of thousand! All this for waiting in the car for half an hour. I didn't know what Rod had done in that house, but I knew that I was onto a winner. I didn't have to threaten anyone, beat anyone up, or verbally berate a soul. My life was not in danger; it was too sweet to be true. This was what I had been seeking all my life – earning easy money, and a lot of it.

8

Broken Dreams

I met up with Rod as much as I could. He was really calculating and knew how to suss out people's weaknesses. He obviously knew mine was the love of money – greed. I'd pester him for work and he'd keep telling me, 'I've got an eye on a job. Something with a large lump of cash.'

'When we going to do it?'

'Soon, mate, soon.'

But 'soon' wasn't soon enough for me. I had dreams and visions of owning my five-bedroomed house in Florida, driving big cars, flashing money around, knowing that I had an endless supply that could never run out.

We did more jobs – some worked out and some didn't. Slowly I was amassing money, fuelled by my thoughts of having it all. One time, we went to a house and searched everywhere for the money we knew was there. We turned over the front room, bedrooms, bathrooms and loft but found nothing. I started to get angry. Then Rod's phone rang.

'Si, the guy's on his way back. He's twenty minutes away.'

'But he was supposed to be away all night.'

'We'd better get out – now.'

'No. I'm not leaving here until I find that money.'

Running down the stairs, I stood in the hallway and waited. My police training had given me 'another sense'; I knew to look for something that was out of place, and maybe that was where the money was hidden. I walked into the kitchen and looked around. I could 'feel' the money; I just had to take my time to work out what was wrong. Then I saw it.

'Nice one,' said Rod.

For this job, I netted a good whack – far beyond my wildest dreams. Back to Florida I went.

The desire for money had intensified. The more I was getting, the more I wanted. I felt I was living 'the dream' – but *still* something was missing. I had everything I'd always wanted, but it still wasn't enough; I couldn't work out what was wrong.

'How much is that, mate?'

'Oh, the Grand Cherokee, black, 4x4, leather interior, blacked out windows, four litres of pure luxury, sir, with the price tag of only £20,000.'

'Right, I'll take it. No need to wrap it up,' I laughed. Never before was I able to go into a showroom, pick out the car of my dreams and pay cash for it. But this was now the way I lived. The only problem was, as quickly as I was 'earning', I was spending. On top of that, I was cranking up my maximum limit on my credit cards. My thinking was that it didn't matter. I was able to steadily pay off the debts on the cards with the illegal money that was coming in through my working relationship with Rod. I was living for today. My hunger and thirst for money was insatiable. I was fully addicted, like any drug addict. I loved holding the money and then salting it away. Whenever I needed it, I would retrieve it and spend it all.

My work with Rod was great, but for me, it wasn't regular enough. I wanted to earn that kind of money every day if possible. Rod was into a lot of things and I wanted him to share more of his ventures with me. So, every day I phoned him, sometimes two or three times a day, begging him to give me more work. I was a man possessed, and the only antidote was – to earn more money!

At the gym one morning, I was lifting weights, trying to work up a sweat when Rod came in.

'Look, Simon,' he said. 'I tell you what I can do for you. I can introduce you to certain people who will be able to help you out. The thing is though, Si, you have to be careful. These people are "real" people. You can't mess 'em about, they won't have it. Cross 'em, and they'll end up sorting you out.' He looked at me straight in the eye as though he wanted to say more, but couldn't.

I was like an eager puppy. 'Yeah, Rod, tell 'em about me, I'm up for anything.'

Shrugging, Rod simply said, 'OK.'

Rod arranged a meeting with me and some guys who I believed would open up the door for me to really earn some serious money. I had dreamt about owning a home in Florida, moving out there permanently with my family and just living off my earnings. Call it early retirement, whatever. When I met these guys I could almost taste the sweet success of the profits that would surely come by my association with them.

There were three guys at the restaurant. It was obvious from the clothes they wore and the way they handled themselves that I was in *serious* company. Vic was top boss. I sussed that out quickly, simply by the way the other guys deferred to him, giving up bundles of respect. I sat facing them and I felt like a small boy in the presence of the toughest boys in the playground.

'I hear you want to do some work for us?' said Vic.

'Yeah, that's right. I'm very hungry. I just want to get busy, you know.'

'Well, you're in luck. There is an opening for you.' He looked at me and I really wanted to ask him where, what, who and why, but I knew that these guys were on a higher level then anyone I had ever had dealings with before. So I stayed quiet.

Vic dipped his hand into his pocket and withdrew a mobile phone. He pushed it in my direction and said, 'We'll give you a call when we're ready to give you some work.' He shook my hand and said, 'It was nice to meet you.' I knew that was my signal to leave. Driving away from the restaurant, I had an overwhelming feeling that I had hit the jackpot.

Within a few days I got a phone call from the guys and I was in business. Over the next couple of months I was collecting and delivering packages on a regular basis. I didn't ask any questions and I was getting about five grand a week for my services.

This was *it* for me. I wasn't getting the large chunks of cash here and there, but a steady five or ten grand that was slowly building up into serious amounts of money. *That* was the way I could live the dream.

It was a Friday night when I got a phone call from Vic calling me to a meeting. Again, it was just the four of us. Vic told me that they were investing in a new venture, bringing a commodity up from southern Spain. I was interested.

'Would you like to come in on the ground level?' he asked.

I didn't hesitate. 'Yes!' Since I had been working with Vic and the guys, I was earning good money and the thought that I could earn more made me jump straight in.

The initial investment was ten grand. That wasn't too much of a hardship for me.

Vic continued. 'If everything goes according to plan you should double the 10K in a couple of weeks.' He was so casual, compared to me. I had to get a grip on myself to appear cool too. I sauntered out of the restaurant when I really want to jump up and kick my heels. This was the pot of gold at the end of the rainbow!

A couple of weeks passed. Then I heard from Vic.

'The deal's come through fine. Your money's safe.'

My options were to take the money, or to leave it in for another run and double it up again. So I left it in the pot, doubling it until I had forty grand in total. Then I was summoned to another meeting.

Vic said, 'Everything seems to be fine. Everything is set up now. Nothing can go wrong. We're all gonna take a leap of faith. We're going to increase our investment to £100,000. Are you with us?'

I knew this was 'make or break' time. Investing so much money would mean that I would have to call on every single penny that I had saved, and plunge it into this scheme. I was feeling a bit worried, but the thought of getting double what I had put in outweighed my fears. Frankly, the hunger for money was so strong that at times I would get breathless just thinking about it. Anyway, I told Vic I was in and handed over the money. By now, I completely trusted Vic; I was going to sit back and wait for the phone call to tell me to come and collect.

I did get a call. But it wasn't what I expected.

'We need to meet up. There's been a problem.'

To begin with, I wasn't too worried. These guys were top brass and they could sort out anything. Or so I thought. I met them, and Vic told me, 'The commodity has been discovered by the Spanish police. The courier has been arrested. The investment's gone, everything has gone pear-shaped.'

'What?' It was as if his words couldn't penetrate my brain. I had come to the meeting expecting to be told that I'd need my holdall to take my investment home. I was numb. It couldn't take it in. Did he mean that I had lost my money? His next words confirmed my fears.

'It looks like we lost it all,' said Vic, coolly.

I was speechless. I saw my house in Florida flash before me, and then it was gone.

'Well, what we gonna do, then?' I said. 'We can't just sit back and wait!'

Shrugging, Vic replied, 'We're gonna send a man down there and see what he can come up with. There's not much else we can do at the moment.'

My mouth was dry and my mind was jumping all over place. I wanted to get up and do something, but what? I knew that £100,000 to them was nothing, but to me it was my *life*. I had risked my life and liberty to get it together and now it was gone. How was I going to get my money back? How was I going to live?

Over the next few days I was ringing them non-stop but my calls were unanswered. So I found out where Vic was and, without waiting for him to grant me a meeting, I just turned up.

'What's going on with my 100K?'

'Look,' said Vic, 'we've made some enquiries – it's gone. Sometimes you gamble, and sometimes you lose. We lost this time.'

'But is there nothing we can do?' I demanded. 'Is there nothing we've got to go on?'

He handed me a small business card. 'That's the only lead we've got.' He looked at me for a moment. 'If you want my advice, leave it alone. We'll get something else going that will earn you a few quid.'

That was it. There was nothing else for me. I was banging my head against a brick wall. But I could not afford to leave it alone. I had to somehow get my money back, and there was only one way I could think of doing that. I had to get to Spain, and fast.

Returning from my fruitless trip, I knew I had been royally ripped off. The money was gone, and I knew I'd never see it again. But what could I do? These guys weren't the sort I could challenge. One-on-one I could sort them out, but collectively, no way. They didn't play fair and I had my wife and kids to think about; I knew I couldn't protect them 24/7. So I had to reluctantly drop the whole thing.

I had paid the top price for my greed. I just hadn't seen the trap that had been laid for me; I fell in with no resistance, no hesitation. The bait was my yearning for money, and now I had lost the lot.

Shaving one morning, I stopped and looked at myself in the mirror. It was hard for me to believe that a short while ago I was a copper, respected by my peers, earning good money *legally*. Really, I'd had a nice life. But now I had become a desperate, dodgy geezer.

I could have got back in with Vic; I could have phoned Rod to see if he had any work for me. But instead, I did what my instincts told me to do. I rang Vic and said they had carved me up. I let him know in no uncertain terms that I didn't want anything to do with him and his guys. He called me a few names, but I switched the mobile off and smashed it up. Bitterness, anger, hatred and revenge – I felt them all. These guys had given me my dream and then destroyed it before my very eyes. I was up to my neck in debt. I'd ramped up all my credit cards, taken loans out . . . and now I had no means of paying anything back. There was no way I could tell Lynda. I just mumbled, 'I've got everything under control. I'm sorting it all out.'

Laurie rang one afternoon. 'I hear you've had a falling out?'

I told him the whole story. I also told him that I wanted to hurt these guys but Laurie replied, 'Look, Simon, I need to keep in with these people. They're putting it around that you've grassed them up.'

I went ballistic. Not only had they robbed me, now they were trying to stitch me up as well! I felt murderous. 'It's not true! The Old Bill are all over me. If I said anything to them, I would put myself right in it.'

I put the phone down. My money had gone, my dreams had been wiped out; most of my police mates had deserted me long ago, and now my criminal mates were disappearing too. I was a man on a desert island, totally alone. It took all my strength to keep a lid on things. I couldn't talk to Lynda, I couldn't talk to anyone. The criminals thought I was going to grass them up, and the police were following me on a daily basis, knowing one of their own had gone bad. I felt like I was strung up between two wild horses; if someone had said 'go' I would have been ripped apart. I would've ended up either in a shallow grave in Epping Forest, or doing a long prison sentence.

But amazingly, that's when Someone threw me a lifeline.

9

Into the Light

Saturday afternoon was a busy time in the gym. On the outside I was looking in peak condition. I was training twice a day to try to get rid of my anger. But on the inside I was mashed up. Bitterness and murder were continuously in my mind, and I was torturing myself by replaying the events that led up to me losing all my money.

Finishing the workout as I was leaving the gym, I saw a guy on the running machine. I knew this guy. Lee had been a very violent criminal – a powerful drug baron in his day. But, now he had become a Christian and his life had changed. We used to take the mickey out of him, calling him Christian this and Christian that. But today, as I looked at him on the machine, something struck me. His face was radiating a peace and tranquillity that I hadn't noticed before. I was really wasted inside; I'd have liked some of that peace. And in that moment, I had a thought: 'Maybe there's something in this God business, if God can change someone like him.'

So I went over to him and struck up a conversation. We exchanged phone numbers and over the next few weeks we met up several times, and spent time chatting about life, faith – and Jesus Christ.

One time I said to Lee, 'Back when I was a copper at Arsenal, I had a big moustache and the boys used to call me The Walrus.'

'No!' he exclaimed. '*You* were The Walrus? You used to chase me over the terraces.'

What an amazing coincidence! Life had brought us together all these years later – and now this guy was the one who was making me ask questions about God, Jesus and having faith.

Lee kept suggesting that I come with him to his church, but going to church wasn't on my list of priorities. All the churches I had been in before had left me feeling empty. Why would *his* church be any different? Still, Lee was very persistent. He suggested that we go one Sunday evening. He said that afterwards he would treat me to a steak meal, so how could I resist? So off I went to his church, Holy Trinity Brompton, in Knightsbridge.

As I walked through the doors, I was hit by an incredible feeling of peace and love, and the sermon was about real issues, things that you could relate to in your own life. Then, at the end, a guy came over and said a prayer with me: his name was Nicky Gumbel. And I made some sort of commitment to Jesus that very evening.

Walking out of the church, I felt different. Incredibly, in that short space of time, from when I first entered the building to the time I left, *something* had happened to me. I felt as though I had been washed on the inside. Those feelings of revenge and hatred had not completely disappeared, but I just *knew* that their hold on me had lessened. I could feel a degree of peace inside me, peace that was soothing the hurts and bitterness.

During the steak meal, Lee kept telling me that I should go on a Christian course called Alpha. So I signed up for the next one.

Lynda was very sceptical about my new-found faith. When I told her that I would be attending a course to find out more about Christianity, she just said, 'How much is it going to cost?'

Once I started the course, I couldn't get enough of it. Every week I was eager to attend and I had so many questions I thought I would drive everyone crazy. What was mind-blowing to me, and what was really driving me along was the reality that I could have a one-to-one relationship with God, through Jesus Christ.

On the course, there was a weekend away. During one meeting Nicky Gumbel, who was leading it, asked for the Spirit of the Lord to come into our lives. I asked for the Spirit to enter my life because I knew that I couldn't be in a relationship with Jesus without some help. To be honest, there were still some things that I was hanging on to, things from the past I couldn't shake off. Bitterness and anger seemed *just* and *right* to me, as people had hurt me badly. I felt I couldn't let them get away with it. But when the Spirit of the Lord entered me, the evil thoughts and intentions of my heart were broken down and I was left with a fantastic sense of love and peace.

I couldn't stay the whole weekend, as I was playing rugby at Twickenham. For me, it was a privilege, an honour, to be given the chance to play in the same stadium as England played their home games. The feeling was sensational, but it was *nothing* to the peace and love that God bestowed on me on Saturday night.

My life was changing. I was a pleasant person to be around.

Slowly the realisation dawned that material things could never ever satisfy you. That truth turned my whole life around.

I was still driving a top-of-the-range Jeep, but now it meant nothing to me. I got rid of it, exchanged it for a small van. Then I found a job, delivering cars. My wife got me another little job delivering soda to newsagents. Every penny went towards paying off my debts.

Attending church was something that I made sure I didn't miss. I learned to pray – not just reciting 'traditional' prayers that didn't mean a thing, but prayers in which I told God how I was feeling, and about all the things that had and were happening to me. I spoke with God as though He were my personal friend. I started to read my Bible, as I was told that not only would I find out about God and His ways, but God would use the Bible to speak to *me*. It was amazing – the words of the Bible would seem to leap off the page, as though they had come alive, and address some particular issue.

As time went on, I was helping and leading other Alpha courses at Holy Trinity. But even though I had become a Christian, there were still problems and situations in my life that I needed to deal with. Over a period of time I felt God 'telling' me that I needed to deal with my finances. This was a thorny subject. I didn't want to face the stark reality of how much I owed. I felt that if I just paid off as much as I could, somehow, someday, I would be free of debt.

But, in response to what I felt God was saying, I called a financial adviser from the endowment company I had borrowed the money from. She looked at the policy and said, 'It's only got a couple of years left to run. Once you've paid off the loan, there might be some money left for you. I'll look into re-mortgaging your house. Right now, you owe £90,000.' She went off to sort it all out for me.

After a couple of days, she was desperately trying to get hold of me. When we next met up, she said, 'Simon,

I can't believe it. That policy has raised over £40,000!' I could see she was stunned. In one hit, I paid off the loan, took a sizable chunk off the mortgage, and cleared off some credit cards. I was stunned myself. How could this happen? Where did it come from? I was left in no doubt about who was behind my windfall!

I'd had a huge void in my life. I had tried to fill it with money, good times, big cars, excitement, mediums, fortune-tellers, self-help books, New Age philosophy. I had thought these things would give me the answer to my empty life, but every single one of them had led me to a dead end. I know this might sound like a cliché, but now I have truly found what I was looking for. I have found unconditional love, the love of Jesus, and it has made me a complete person. I have found a friend who is always there for me, who won't talk about me behind my back, who won't stitch me up with a dodgy deal. Jesus has always got my best interests at heart.

I haven't become weaker since I became a Christian, I have become stronger. It takes a real man to be humble before the Lord and put off his old ways and life for Jesus. Life is not easy; trials and temptations still come my way. I sometimes read rubbish in the papers, or watch rubbish on TV . . . I even find myself watching Spurs from time to time! But I know now that if I stumble and fall, which I do every single day in thought, word and deed, if I truly repent, I have the loving arms of Jesus to lift me back up.

Through the Alpha course, I did an interview for the BBC with the late John Peel. This was broadcast on Radio 4 at nine o'clock on a Saturday morning. I was amazed at the amount of people who heard it. I was in the gym a few mornings later when Rod came up to me. He said, 'I've heard you found the light?'

'Yeah, I found some faith.'

He smiled. 'We don't have anything to worry about, do we?'

'No, Rod,' I replied. 'I've found my forgiveness in other ways.'

We shook hands and he left.

Not long after meeting up with Rod, I got a phone call from someone who was still in the police force. He said, 'I've heard you've found God?'

'That's right, I found some faith.'

Do you know what he said? 'We don't have anything to worry about, do we?'

I laughed to myself. 'No, mate, I've found my forgiveness in other ways.'

And now . . .

Lee kept telling me that I should come to a prayer meeting that was held by some guys who called themselves Tough Talk. Eventually I went along and I found a group of men, who, like me, had been through the mangle of life. Some were ex-doormen, ex-villians, world champion power-lifters, yet they all had one thing in common – God had made a difference in their lives, and they were using their stories to bring a difference to other people's lives. I started going out with Tough Talk and sharing my story of how God changed my life. I have been amazed at how God uses me to relate to other people and bring them hope – He has turned my life around, and can surely do the same for others.

Being part of Tough Talk has enabled me to travel to France, Spain, Germany, Ireland, Northern Ireland, Scotland and Wales and many, many places in England, sharing the good news of Jesus Christ. My faith has constantly been built up through what I have experienced in the Tough Talk meetings.

If anyone had told me back when I was a police officer, kicking in doors on dodgy council estates, that I would be sharing a stage with ex-doormen and villains, telling people about what Jesus has done in my life, I would have flung them in a cell and thrown away the key – only God could put this together!

The first prison I went into without wearing a police uniform was with the team from Tough Talk. We were setting up the weights, and I felt fine, no problem. Then, the inmates began to come into the gym, about two hundred of them. These were hard men and I was going to have to tell them that I used to be a copper.

I started by saying, 'I was a police officer for twenty-three years . . .' I couldn't get any further. The place erupted with shouts of 'What are you doing here?', 'Scum, copper, get out of here!' and I got a bit fearful. Looking behind me for support, I saw Ian McDowell backing towards the exit! I was tempted to join him. But I carried on and, at the end, I received a standing ovation, and many inmates came and shook my hand. You know what? It's been the same in every prison since! I couldn't do this by myself – I'd be eaten alive. God does this work through me, and the other Tough Talk guys.

A young lad came on the Alpha course. He had a cannabis habit that was taking all his money. His self-esteem was at rock bottom. He loathed himself, hated what he had become – paranoid because of his drug addiction.

Observing him each week as he attended the course, I witnessed the fact that he was slowly able to open up about himself. This young lad was able to begin to talk about what was troubling him. But it was during the

Alpha weekend that a noticeable change occurred. When he was prayed for, the Spirit of the Lord entered him and it seemed as if, in an instant, his face changed – *he* changed. It was unbelievable.

Now, he is able to confidently articulate his feelings, and the drug addiction that had taken over his life is broken. He is free.

This young man is my youngest son, Jamie.

One morning, I was watching the *God Channel* and Joyce Meyer, an evangelist, was speaking about forgiveness and how, if you are holding resentment and unforgiveness inside, you can't go on with God. I didn't think anything about it at the time. That evening, I came home and the *God Channel* was on, and guess what? Exactly the same point was being spoken by Joyce Meyer again. I thought, 'She must be talking to me!' And I realised that I was holding some resentment and unforgiveness against my father from when I was a child.

I knew this had to be sorted out. So I went to see him, forgave him, hugged him and told him I loved him. Two months later, he was diagnosed with leukaemia. He was due to go into hospital for treatment, and I went to see him again. This time, I found a very frightened man. I asked him if I could do something which I had never done before. I asked him if I could pray with him. To my surprise, he said yes.

I hugged my mum and dad and prayed with them. Dad then prayed a simple prayer with me, asking Jesus into his life, and I saw that he was filled with a peace that you can only get from Jesus.

Dad suffered with this disease for twenty months before he died. But I knew that he died with the love and strength of Jesus around him, and that I will see my dad again one day.

On both of these occasions, I had felt God saying to me, 'Bring these people to Me, Simon, and I will make them whole.' And He did.

Although I've changed, my love of football remains the same, and I still love eating in nice restaurants. Florida is still my destination of choice (I've now got a week's timeshare there). But I enjoy my life much more now that I know Jesus as my Lord and Saviour – money is no longer my god. The love and craving for money has left me and I've got different dreams now. I want to be closer to God and more like Jesus. I haven't found 'religion' – I have found a personal relationship with Jesus.

If God can use people like me, and the other members of Tough Talk, think what He could do with *your* life – if you give Him the chance!

Epilogue

You have now read the stories of Joe, Martyn and Simon. The question we would like to put to you is this: Are we telling the truth?

If you believe we are telling the truth – that our stories of how Jesus Christ has changed our lives are real – then the gospel, the good news about Jesus, must be true. The gospel of God's Son is for everybody. No matter how bad or how good you are, we all make mistakes before God. Jesus said 'Anyone who says, "You fool!" will be in danger of the fire of hell' (Matthew 5:22). God's standards are different from ours. There is a way that seems right to humankind, yet that way leads to death (see Proverbs 14:12). Romans 6:23 says, 'The wages of sin is death, but the gift of God is eternal life.' This is the good news:

> For God so loved the world that he gave his one and only Son, that whoever believes in him shall not perish but have eternal life.
>
> (John 3:16)

If you feel this is for you, here is a simple prayer you can say:

> Dear Lord Jesus, I am sorry for the wrong things I have done in my life.
> I believe that you died on the cross for me and took away all my sins. I believe that you rose from the dead and are alive today. Please forgive me and come into my life.
> Thank you Jesus.
> Amen

If you would like to know more about Jesus, please feel free to contact our office by email or letter. It would be great to hear from you. If you are a Christian church, organization or a prison and would like to book Tough Talk for a meeting, our details are below.

**Tough Talk
Brickfield Business Centre,
Brickfield House, High Road,
Thornwood, Epping
CM16 6TH**

**Email: admin@tough-talk.com
Phone: 01992 566785
Website: www.tough-talk.com**